Your Towns and Cities in the

Sunderland
in the Great War

Your Towns and Cities in the Great War

Sunderland
in the Great War

Clive Dunn and Gillian Dunn

Pen & Sword
MILITARY

First published in Great Britain in 2014 by
PEN & SWORD MILITARY
an imprint of
Pen and Sword Books Ltd
47 Church Street
Barnsley
South Yorkshire S70 2AS

Copyright © Clive Dunn and Gillian Dunn, 2014

ISBN 978 1 78346 286 5

Printed and bound in England
by Page Bros, Norwich

Typeset in Times New Roman

Pen & Sword Books Ltd incorporates the imprints of
Pen & Sword Archaeology, Atlas, Aviation, Battleground, Discovery,
Family History, History, Maritime, Military, Naval, Politics, Railways,
Select, Social History, Transport, True Crime, and Claymore Press,
Frontline Books, Leo Cooper, Praetorian Press, Remember When,
Seaforth Publishing and Wharncliffe.
For a complete list of Pen and Sword titles please contact
Pen and Sword Books Limited
47 Church Street, Barnsley, South Yorkshire, S70 2AS, England
E-mail: enquiries@pen-and-sword.co.uk
Website: **www.pen-and-sword.co.uk**

Contents

Foreword

WE HAVE WRITTEN this book to commemorate the part Sunderland played in the Great War, not only in supplying men and women to the armed forces but also in the contribution of its industry and the men who were not able to go to the front and women on the home front made to the war effort. We have been aided greatly by one of the wartime mayors, William Frederick Vint, who wrote *A Mayor's Notebook*. We would especially like to thank the staff at the Local Studies Centre of Sunderland Library for their time, patience and help.

Sunderland Coat of Arms.

Chapter One

1914: The calm before the storm
Patriotism, proclamations and preparations

SUNDERLAND HAD PROSPERED during the nineteenth and early twentieth centuries as a shipbuilding town and producer of coal, pottery and glass. The early part of 1914 had seen an escalation of international tensions with the continued naval arms race between the Germany of Kaiser Wilhelm II and Great Britain. On 28 June 1914, during a state visit to Sarajevo, Archduke Franz Ferdinand and his wife Sophie, the Duchess of Hohenberg, were assassinated by Gavrilo Princip, a member of the Serbian Black Hand Gang. After this, events rapidly moved towards war, although this was not known at the time. Austria was eager for war and, with the knowledge that Germany would support her, sent a harsh ultimatum to Serbia, knowing full well that the Serbians would not agree to it. In the event Serbia agreed to most of the points raised, but not all. This partial acceptance was not enough for Austria-Hungary. As a consequence, it invaded Serbia.

Europe at this time was divided into an armed camp, with Germany and Austria-

A general view of High Street, Sunderland.

Hungary on one side and France and Russia on the other. Great Britain initially took the view that it did not want to be drawn into a European war, but that was a hope that would not be fulfilled. With the invasion of Serbia, Russia mobilized her forces on 31 July. Germany then sent an ultimatum to Russia stating that if the latter did not stop mobilization then it too would be forced to mobilize its forces and declare a state of war. At the same time, Germany informed France of its intentions towards Russia and wanted to know what France would do; would it remain neutral? The Russians did not reply to Germany's ultimatum so, on 1 August 1914, Germany declared war. On the same day, France mobilized its troops. The next day, German troops invaded Luxemburg and that night a note was sent to the Belgian government stating that the latter must violate Belgian territory and demanded that Belgium remained neutral. This note required an answer within twelve hours. The Belgians sent their refusal by 7.00 am on 3 August. Later that day, Germany declared war on France. The next day, Britain lodged protests with Germany about its invasion of Belgium and sent her an ultimatum to safeguard Belgian neutrality. When no reply was received Britain declared war on Germany at 11.00 pm on 4 August.

While all this was happening, the people of Sunderland were following events avidly, with life still going on as normal, this being a bank holiday weekend. The War Office issued the following statement on 4 August: 'With reference to this [Monday] afternoon's announcement of the government of their decision to mobilize. It is officially stated that the proclamation will be signed to-day, and the necessary orders for the Reserves to return to the colours and the Territorials to be embodied will then be issued.' War was in the air.

That night at midnight, thousands of people crowded around the *Echo* offices in Bridge Street, Sunderland, awaiting developments. All copies of the special edition of the

newspaper quickly sold out as people clamoured for news. Shortly after midnight, word came that a state of war existed between Great Britain and Germany. At first there was silence while people took in the gravity of the situation; then there was a cheer, and people dispersed to their homes singing the national anthem.

With the start of the first full day of war things began happening in the town. There was an expectancy that the war would be over by Christmas but also the worry that the Germans may invade the country. Britain had traditionally relied upon the Royal Navy to protect her shores from invasion. However, an exercise in 1913 to test the defences of England proved

General Post Office.

View from Wearmouth Bridge.

that it would be possible for an enemy to land the equivalent of 48,000 troops between Blyth and Sunderland before the Navy could intervene. This prompted a lot of rethinking in the planning circles. The War Office took over the grain warehouses at the South Docks and other places such as the Thompson Memorial Hall, Pilot House on the north pier, the café on the lower promenade and Mrs Just's premises on the lower promenade.

The local Territorial Force battalion, 7/Durham Light Infantry, were away at camp, at Conway in North Wales, with the rest of the Durham Light Infantry Brigade. Camp was interrupted with the announcement that the country was at war and all units had to return home. This came as a shock to some of those serving. Private Joe Robson of C Company 7/Durham Light Infantry later recalled:

We were all settled down for the camp when at 3 o'clock in the morning of 4 August the buglers sounded reveille. War was declared. We were mobilized. Orders were issued to get your gear on, full pack and 250 rounds of ammunition. The cooks had been woken up and they did what they could for us before we left. They were cooking meat and potatoes. They put a potato in one hand a lump of meat in the other and we were then shoved into the train. We came straight back to Sunderland arriving about 6 o'clock; we had been on the train from about 4 o'clock that morning. When we arrived back at Sunderland we were marched back to the Garrison Field at Livingston Road.

A Pierrot concert at Roker before the war.

Crowds greeted the return of the battalion. The battalion marched back to the Drill Hall at Livingstone Road, now the site of the Gill Bridge Police station, where they awaited further instructions. Some thought that they would be going straight to the front to fight the Germans. At that time the Territorial Force was for home defence only.

Private Robson continues his story:

We stood around for about two hours; they did not know what to do with us. We were just young lads wondering what we were going to do; we thought we were going straight to war. The CO sent out some men to get bottles of beer, bottles of pop or sandwiches or a pie. When they came back I had a pie and a bottle of pop. This was about 9 o'clock, we were absolutely worn out with our packs on. We grounded

**Private Joe Robson,
C Company, 7/Durham
Light Infantry.**

Conway camp, 7/Durham Light Infantry.

our rifles until we had eaten our food. We had just finished when it must have been about 10 o'clock, the commander got in front of us on his horse and said, 'You can all go home but don't take your clothes off; you can be called up any minute.'

We were glad to get home; 'course it was all trams then. I lived in St Lukes Terrace at this time. My mother was a widow. I had lost my father when I was two years old. She used to look after me. When I got home I told my mother we've got to keep our clothes on, we might be called up at any minute.

So I took my pack off my back, my pouches with the 250 rounds of ammunition and water bottle, and laid them on the floor. I did not take my tunic or trousers off. I took my boots off and put my slippers on. I lay on the settee all night and nobody came. Nobody came the next day. I thought I would be at home for a while so I

General view of Conway camp in August 1914, where the Territorials spent their fortnight's training.

decided I'll go to bed that night. I was just going to get ready, I was worn out, it was about 9 o'clock and they came round and said we had to report to the Garrison Field.

The troops were deployed according to a prearranged plan around the town guarding vital installations such as the docks and bridges. The whole of the Northumbrian Division was deployed along the coast, from South Shields to the Tees. Crowds used to go to Roker to watch the troops dig trenches, which formed part of the coastal defence. Some of the earth from the trenches was used to strengthen earthworks at Abbs Point Battery. Although there was a novelty about the troops and what they were doing, there was also a serious side to things. No one could enter the docks without a pass. Some people out for an evening walk received a shock when they were challenged by a sentry with a bayonet fixed to his rifle when they got too close to any defences. Other restrictions had an effect on the town's population. By order of the military the electric lights on Roker Promenade were switched off and would not be turned on again without further orders. The steps leading down to Hendon Beach were removed. However, the locals did help to look after the troops. When it became known that the garrison of Seaburn Farm had not eaten that day because their rations had not arrived, they made sandwiches for them.

But it was not just on land that incidents happened. On the evening of 9 August, the Scottish collier SS *Startforth* on entering the harbour was challenged by a sentry on the pier. No reply was returned so the sentry turned out the guard, who fired a volley at the ship, wounding two on board. James Holmes Jackson was shot in the leg and his thigh was broken. When the ship docked he was taken to hospital. The other casualty, Matthew Ross, the captain, was only slightly injured. In their defence, the crew claimed they had replied to the sentry, but their reply had not been heard.

There was excitement when the local heavy battery of the Durham Royal Garrison Artillery took their 4.7-inch guns through the town to Cleadon Hills to form part of the defences, both against raids from the sea and also from the air.

Adverts now started to appear for recruits. One for the Royal Naval Air Service asked for men of between eighteen and thirty years of age who 'should have experience of one or more of the following: (a) general upkeep, construction or repair of aircraft; (b) carpenter's work, joinery, cabinet making; (c) boat building; (d) fabric work (airship or aeroplane); (e) fitting and turning; (f) care, maintain and repair of petrol engines; (g) coppersmith's work; (h) electrician's work; (i) cycle mechanics; (j) motor driving.' As the war progressed some of these qualifications would have been relaxed with on-the-job training.

Sunderland had its own barracks, which had been built during the middle of the nineteenth century. At this time they were not used as such and the houses there were let. People living in those houses were now told to find other accommodation as soon as possible as the barracks were to be taken over by the military again.

Just prior to the declaration of war the Royal Navy deployed to its war stations, the main part of the fleet going to Scapa Flow in the Orkneys. The Navy was faced with a new menace: that of submarines. Early in the war one U-boat managed to enter Scapa Flow, which caused a certain amount of panic. To combat this threat, blockships were sunk in strategic places. Two such had been built in Sunderland: the 2,418-ton steamer SS *Almeria* and the 1,941-ton steel single-screw steamer SS *Rhonda*, built in 1888 and 1889 respectively. In addition to blockships the Navy used anti-submarine nets. The SS

A destroyer built in 1896, typical of the pre-war naval ships produced on the Wear.

Rhonda was kept in position throughout the Second World War as well, but was considered a hazard to shipping and was blown up in 1962.

Forward planning was also taking place. The 6 and 12 Durham Volunteer Aid Detachments (VAD) began to look for premises for temporary hospitals, in anticipation of casualties. In consequence of the generous nature of the town's people, two hospitals were formed. The 6/VAD hospital was at the Jeffrey Memorial Hall, Monk Street, and the 12/VAD hospital was at Gray Road. Mrs Ernest Vaux and Mrs Ernest Wright were quartermasters of the latter. Mrs Vaux was the wife of Lieutenant Colonel Ernest Vaux, commanding officer of 7/Durham Light Infantry. Volunteer Aid Detachments came about following the Boer War, when it was thought that in the event of a major European war the peacetime army medical services would not be able to cope with the expected influx of casualties. The Territorial Force came into being on 1 April 1908, and on 16 August 1909, the War Office issued a 'Scheme for the Organization of Voluntary Aid in England and Wales', which set up both male and female Voluntary Aid Detachments around the country. The size of detachments varied but mainly consisted of a commandant, medical officer, quartermaster and twenty-two women, two of whom were nurses. The roll of the

HMS *Haughty*, a 27-knott A Class destroyer, built at Doxford's in 1895.

VADs was to staff auxiliary hospitals and convalescent stations. Pre-war training consisted of a minimum of one meeting per month, where basic first aid was taught. The VAD organization was run by the Joint War Committee of the British Red Cross Society and the Order of St John.

Other things were happening in the town. The police had received instructions from the military to arrest all Germans capable of bearing arms. On 8 August, a large crowd gathered to watch the proceedings when sixty Germans were brought in. In addition to these measures enemy vessels in the harbour were detained, but it was hoped that the government would come to an arrangement for the exchange of vessels held by the Central Powers. While these measures were taking place in Sunderland, similar things were happening in Europe. Captain Sydney Butchart, of Thornhill Gardens in Sunderland, tried to join his ship at Trieste, Austria, which was on passage to India. He arrived after war had been declared and was prevented from boarding; instead he had to return home by rail. During the journey he had some unpleasant experiences, one of which being that his luggage was confiscated, as had been the case with a lot of other travellers. Needless to say, Captain Butchart was glad to get back home to Sunderland. Captain Butchart was a member of the River Wear Watch Commissioners; he died on 20 October 1916 at the grand old age of seventy-three.

On 12 August, Lord Kitchener issued his famous appeal for men for six divisions for the duration of the war. It was also becoming apparent that men from all occupations throughout the town were leaving to join either the colours or the Territorials. The Gas Company announced it would keep positions open for any of their employees called up and that they would make up any difference in pay. Likewise, eleven tramway men were called up and it was expected another fifteen were to go. The tram company said that normal service would continue, but people were not to expect any special services to run.

With a number of policemen either being called back to the colours, being mobilized as part of the Territorial Force or simply joining up, the Home Secretary was becoming concerned for the preservation of law and order throughout the country. A circular was issued to all local authorities with the aim of recruiting a force of unpaid special constables. The force was to consist of those men who were either too old or unable to serve in the Army, Navy or Territorial Force and who were desirous of serving their country. Steps were taken to start the recruitment and to allocate the men to various districts within the town. It was emphasized that the new force was not to be considered town guards or civil guards, but to form part of the police force. An appeal from Cecil F. De Pledge, Chairman of the Local Emergency Committee, to the local newspaper was made for suitable persons:

> I wish to point out that one of the principal and most important duties of special constables, in the event of any emergency arising, will be to prevent and allay alarm which may be excited and to direct inhabitants as to the course to be pursued. It is therefore essential that well-known and responsible gentlemen should act in that office and I invite all our public men, leading tradesmen, school teachers and others whose influence would have weight with the inhabitants generally at once to enrol, in order that the organization may be completed and everyone be instructed in time as to the duties assigned to him and the district assigned for his operations.

An article appeared in the *Jewish Chronicle* stating that Jews had been refused permission to be special constables and that those who had already been accepted would be issued with letters asking them to return their papers. It was thought that this was outrageous, especially as the country was in such peril.

Other organizations were having difficulties with the loss of adult members. The Boys' Brigade lost eight out of thirty adult volunteers to the forces. It was deemed necessary for battalion weekly route marches through the town and surrounding areas instead of the usual company size contingent. As well as this, the officers and older lads joined together to form stretcher bearer parties to help in times of emergencies.

Warnings were beginning to appear that prices would start going up as a result of the declaration of war. One such, which affected almost everyone, concerned gas mantles. As most houses had gas lighting and because most gas mantles came from Germany, it was reported that stocks were now low, which they had been even at the outbreak of war, therefore, it was predicted that the prices would rise by twenty per cent. Shopkeepers in the town were trying to keep their prices down as long as their stock lasted but said that they would have to go up later.

Recruiting was a big issue in the town, with all regiments and both services seeking men. A letter from Mr Greenwood MP was published in the *Sunderland Echo* comparing the town with Liverpool. He pointed out that whereas Liverpool had a population four times greater than Sunderland, they had taken four weeks to recruit 1,000 men, whereas Sunderland had raised 1,100 within three weeks. He went on to say that the recruiting stations at John Street and Havelock House, Roker, were very busy.

A meeting was held on 4 September at the Subscription Library in Fawcett Street to bring some organization to the recruiting efforts within the town. It was agreed following a proposal by Colonel Barker that a committee should be formed. Mr William Morrison was appointed chairman, with Messrs J.A. Raine and N.J. Brotherton as joint secretaries.

Fawcett Street.

A sub-committee was also organized to arrange for speakers and for motor cars that would take the speakers to the various venues and then to take recruits to the recruiting offices. It was initially proposed to hold small meetings, with bigger meetings being planned for later. Both the Wearmouth Colliery Band and the East End Band promised their assistance.

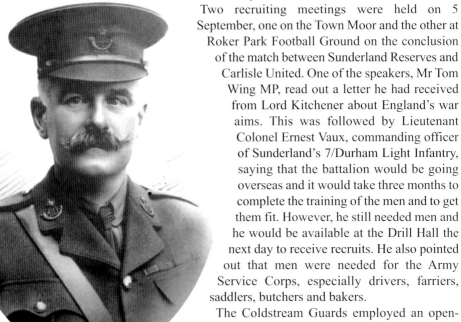

Lieutenant Colonel Ernest Vaux, commanding officer of 7/Durham Light Infantry.

Two recruiting meetings were held on 5 September, one on the Town Moor and the other at Roker Park Football Ground on the conclusion of the match between Sunderland Reserves and Carlisle United. One of the speakers, Mr Tom Wing MP, read out a letter he had received from Lord Kitchener about England's war aims. This was followed by Lieutenant Colonel Ernest Vaux, commanding officer of Sunderland's 7/Durham Light Infantry, saying that the battalion would be going overseas and it would take three months to complete the training of the men and to get them fit. However, he still needed men and he would be available at the Drill Hall the next day to receive recruits. He also pointed out that men were needed for the Army Service Corps, especially drivers, farriers, saddlers, butchers and bakers.

The Coldstream Guards employed an open-topped tram to attract recruits. The Guards' band went through the town to Havelock House, Roker, on this specially decorated tram, playing stirring marches. It was quite a success as a lot of men followed the procession. At the same time, Major Marr of the Durham Heavy Battery Royal Garrison Artillery, which as mentioned had its guns on Cleadon Hills, needed a further 130 men to bring the unit up to wartime establishment. He was given permission to march through the principal parts of the town to the Drill Hall on The Green.

Recruiting in the town started to become busier. The Recruiting Office in John Street was moved to the upper floor of the County Court to cope. It was announced that during the week prior to 5 September, Major Byrne and his staff had recruited 3,447 men and as an experiment their offices had opened on Sunday, when forty-four men joined. The next day, a further 381 signed up.

A report of the death on 31 August of a Sunderland recruit, Gunner Joseph Lewins, Royal Garrison Artillery, was published in the *Sunderland Echo* on 2 September. He had previously worked as a labourer at the docks and came from 50 Hendon Street; he had joined a week earlier. He had been sent to Newhaven, where he had been engaged in transport work. It was reported that he had been found with his throat cut, but it was not certain how this had happened. He left a wife and one son.

As previously mentioned, English ships that happened to be in enemy ports when war was declared had been impounded and it was considered that the men aboard may be treated as prisoners of war. However, a number of ships also carried women. One such was ship owners Messrs Westoll's boat, *President*. Aboard was Mrs Errington, the wife of the captain, her daughter, sister-in-law and a friend. The ship had sailed from Sunderland, on its regular run, with a cargo of coal to Hamburg. It arrived on the afternoon war had been declared between Russia and Germany. The cargo had been unloaded but the ship had not been allowed to leave. The women had been permitted to move around Hamburg as they liked for four days, then they had been confined to the ship with the men. Living conditions had been comfortable, but they only had provisions for a week. The Germans were able to supplement these, much to the relief of all on board. The women were then given permission to write to the head of the Hamburg police, who in turn gave his permission for them to return to England, via the Netherlands. They arrived back in Sunderland on 26 August.

On 16 August, the first elements of the British Army arrived in France to be warmly greeted by the inhabitants. Private Hindmarch, of the Coldstream Guards, wrote to his mother to say that he had landed at Le Havre to a warm welcome from the French. There were plenty of apples and pears in the area where he was billeted and it seemed like the whole countryside was an orchard, especially as it was harvest time.

Patriotism was running at an all-time high in Sunderland. The workmen at Messrs Pickergill's agreed to deduct 2d in the pound per week to go to the Lord Lieutenant's Relief Fund for the county. This generous gesture was followed by other workmen in other firms throughout the town. The Secretary of the Wear Shipbuilders' Association said that those apprentices who enlisted would be considered as being on a leave of absence for a period of not exceeding twelve months. The time would be considered as part of the apprenticeship. If they were away for more than twelve months the matter would be given further consideration, which is what happened.

On a sadder note, the number of inmates at the workhouse in Chester Road had risen by 100 since the start of the war. No specific reason had been given for this. According to the 1881 Census, the workhouse had 699 inmates and it was shortly after the turn of the century that it was expanded to cater for more people, and by 1911 there were 1,220 inmates. The Highfield Cottage Homes were erected to the north of the site to provide accommodation for small families. Each cottage was supervised by a house 'father' or 'mother'.

During the first weekend of September, the Boy Scouts paraded through the town. A total of 580 were on parade, comprising seventeen troops and a troop of Wolf Cubs. The whole parade marched from the Garrison Field to Christ Church. The Scouts did feel an element of disappointment because it had been hoped that the parade would have been commanded by Lieutenant General R.S. Baden-Powell, but unfortunately he was called to London, virtually at the last moment, on war business. The parade was instead commanded by Major Cuthbert Vaux.

It was not only the men who were called to the colours on the outbreak of war; nurses were also mobilized. As a result, from the Royal Victoria Infirmary, Sister Logan and Nurse McKay were sent to Chatham Royal Naval Hospital; Nurse Swales and Sister Lumsden went to the Royal Herbert Military Hospital, Woolwich; and Nurses Walker and Browning to the Military Hospital, Colchester. The matron of the Royal Victoria Infirmary received the following letter from the War Office:

Madam,

I shall be gratefully obliged if in the event of your having a surplus of nurses belonging to your present nursing staff who would be available for service, you would kindly inform me of the fact, as I am desirous of knowing where I can procure reliable nurses at short notice. This supply would be additional to the nurses already guaranteed by your hospital to the War Office, and should not include any army nurses who are not actually with you at present, as I am already in correspondence with many who were formerly in your training school.

E.H. Betcher, Matron-in-Chief QAIMNS
[Queen Alexandria's Imperial Military Nursing Service]

Also during early September there was a spate of attacks on shops purportedly owned by Germans. On the evening of 7 September, at the corner of North Bridge Street and Howick Street, Monkwearmouth, a window of pork butcher Mr A. Hellier's shop was broken. A man had left the shop and then threw a bottle as hard as he could through a plate-glass window and then ran off. A large crowd quickly gathered but no further damage was done to the shop, although one or two windows were broken in houses in Howick Street. Children were blamed for that damage. The police soon dispersed the crowd but the man who threw the bottle was not caught.

The next day, Eugene F. Lang's, pork butchers of The Terrace, Southwick, had six windows broken by a woman using her shoe. Later during the month a shipwright by the name of George Henry Bailes was charged with drunkenness and wilful damage. It was alleged, at the Magistrates Court, that Bailes had gone to John Conrad Kaufmann's pork butcher's shop in Bridge Street on the afternoon of 15 September, after spending the afternoon drinking, three times to ask for Mr Kaufmann. He was told each time that Mr Kaufmann was out. Shortly after Bailes left for the third time he returned carrying a workman's toolbox. When he was in front of the window, he turned towards it and lurched at it, thereby breaking the glass. Bailes then ran off up the street but was apprehended. In court he claimed it was an accident. Mr Kaufmann's counsel stated that Mr Kaufmann was an Englishman born and bred, with an English wife, and that he only employed Englishmen. Bailes was subsequently sent for trial at the sessions. A follow-up to this story is that Mr Kaufmann's window was broken again, the next day. A man ran head-first at it and broke the window to pieces, running off, but was eventually caught. Alexander Cruickshanks was arrested by special constables Greenlay and Watson for this latest incident. The damaged he caused amounted to £13 11s 3d. Cruickshanks was caught in Matlock Street, still bleeding from his head and both hands. He was later committed for trial. It was said that he had done this following another incident at Kaufmann's pork butcher's when Joseph Johnson, who was the worse for drink, had gone into the shop and ordered a three-penny pork sandwich. He took it and left the shop, refusing to pay for it. Mr Kaufmann followed him out and accosted Johnson in the street, this incident being witnessed by Cruickshanks.

Another report on recruiting appeared from Major Byrne on 7 September, stating that 1,205 men had enlisted, the majority being miners. It was also announced by the War Office that those who enlisted for three years, or the duration of the war, except for the Royal Engineers, would serve for one day with the colours and then be transferred to the Reserve until the depots throughout the country were ready to receive them. Due to the large influx of recruits, following Lord Kitchener's appeal and for other patriotic reasons, the depots were congested and could not cope with any more. The War Office also requested that speakers at rallies ask potential recruits not to present themselves for a week at least. This would allow the authorities to catch up with their work and to organize clothing, billets and feeding arrangements.

The War Office had issued an appeal for ex-non-commissioned officers to help train the new 'Kitchener's Army'. The appeal was for ex-warrant officers and sergeants up to fifty years of age and junior NCOs up to the age of forty-five. If they had been an ex-Regular soldier they would be promoted to the rank they held on discharge, up to the rank of sergeant. Those who rejoined and were over forty-five years old would be used for home service only. On re-enlistment they would receive a gratuity of £10 for overseas service and £5 for home service. Most of these men would be employed as instructors.

Following a parade in September through Sunderland, the Durham Royal Garrison Artillery heavy battery was nearly up to its wartime strength.

Not only were men and women joining the colours but local organizations were being formed. At a meeting at the YMCA it was decided to form an athletics force, and a committee was formed to see this through. The new force had been able to obtain the services of two ex-Army drill instructors. Drill was to take place on the Sunderland West End Football Field, where they would be taught the rudiments of rifle shooting and drill. Offers of the use of Hendon Cricket Club, Sunderland Rovers Club and Sunderland West End Club grounds were received. In addition, the Athletes' Volunteer Force, as it became known, also had the use of St Gabriel's Hall and St Columba's Hall for drill nights, which were to take place on Tuesdays and Thursdays between 7.30 pm and 9.00 pm. This force eventually rose to 285 members under the command of Captain T.T. Nesbitt and was later formed into companies for different parts of the town. Later, rumours started to circulate that the Athletes' Volunteer Force may receive official recognition. A meeting was held at the Guildhall, London, comprising representatives of various forces throughout the country. Mr S. Curle and Captain Nesbitt represented Sunderland. When the two men returned to the town after the meeting, they reported that the impression received of official recognition was unfounded. The authorities stated that they shortly intended to issue regulations to each force, which would make clear the position as to official recognition. At the beginning of December it was decided to form a fifth company from Millfield and district, based at Franklin Street Schoolroom, and a change of emphasis for the Volunteer Force. Young men between the ages of sixteen and nineteen would be trained with a view to transferring to the forces when needed. Joining members were to contribute 6d a month to meet expenses.

Around this time, Sunderland Football Club started drilling at Roker Park. Some thirty people were on parade, including all the players, with the exception of George Holley. The parade was taken by W.H. Bell, the vice chairman of the club, who was an ex-captain in the Sunderland Artillery Volunteers. The parade lasted for an hour, and everyone seemed to enjoy themselves.

Mentioned earlier was the breaking of pork butcher Mr Hellier's window. A few days later, Mr Hellier, along with Pastor Hertzog, a ship's fireman, and other prominent pork butcher's in the town were arrested by the police because they were German Reservists. They were taken into custody, pending internment.

Recruiting started to take a different angle, in line with the rest of the country, in forming Pals battalions. Permission had now been received from Lord Kitchener for the county to raise a battalion of professional men (including artisans) for the Durham Light Infantry. In the same way as other Pals battalions, they would be kept together as far as possible. The battalion would be equipped by public subscription, most of which had been guaranteed. The men would enlist for the duration of the war, or not exceeding three years. Men between the ages of nineteen and thirty-five (for officers the upper age limit was fifty-five), with a chest measurement of not less than 35$^{1/2}$ inches, height not less than 5 feet 6 inches, were needed. This battalion recruited throughout the county; in Sunderland, the enrolment offices were at Somerford Buildings, under the direction of Mr J. Morley Longden. An advertisement subsequently appeared in the *Sunderland Echo* for 'Commercial men and those who wish to join with their personal friends'.

Tragedy happened on 5 September when HMS *Pathfinder*, a scout cruiser, had the distinction of being the first warship to be sunk by a torpedo fired by a submarine during the war. The torpedo, fired from the U21, hit the forward magazine, causing it to explode. From a crew of 570, only seventy survived. Amongst those who lost their lives was a Sunderland man by the name of Thomas Cooper, from Monkwearmouth. He is commemorated on the Chatham Naval Memorial.

HMS *Pathfinder*, on which Thomas Cooper served.

Another sailor, James McCulloch, on HMS *Bristol*, wrote to his mother at The Gray School House, stating that 'We were the first to fire, sixteen hours after war was declared. We were fighting one of the Germans for half an hour and she had to fly. We got the best of her, though we only hit her a few times. … They say the first ship to fire is to get a gold medal, so I think we have a chance.' No such medal was issued. The ship James McCulloch refers to is probably the SMS *Karlsruhe*, which HMS *Bristol* had a short skirmish with on 6 August.

Following the declaration of war on 4 August, the British Army had been completing its mobilization plans. The first contingent of the British Expeditionary Force (BEF), under the command of Sir John French, landed in France on 16 August, following a prearranged plan with the French. Quite a number of Sunderland men, ex-Regular soldiers, had been recalled to the colours and therefore formed part of the BEF. By 20 August, the BEF had completed its concentration in the area of Avesnes and Le Cateau and the next day they started a move forward towards the Belgian town of Mons. It was here on 23 August that the first battle between the British and Germans took place, with the British holding the canal at Mons and digging in to stop the German advance. During the battle that followed the BEF held the Germans on their front due to the 'mad minute', the firing of fifteen aimed shots within a minute, which every infantryman had been trained for, and the excellent cover provided by the guns of the Artillery. The Germans, however, greatly outnumbered the BEF and were coming around their left flank while the French Fifth Army retired on their right flank, without informing Sir John French. In order not to be cut off and overwhelmed, the BEF was forced to start their retirement towards the Marne, near Paris, in what was to become known as the Retreat from Mons.

It was shortly after the Battle of Mons that letters started arriving back in Sunderland giving details of what was happening in France. Private J. Lauder, C Company Gordon Highlanders, wrote to his parents telling them of the narrow escape he had had at Mons. A piece of shrapnel or a bullet had made a hole in his water bottle, but luckily he was not hurt. He mentioned that this was worse than the Boer War.

A number of telegrams arrived reporting men missing. Lance Corporal James William Holyoak and Private Harry Gillespie, of 5 Bishopton Street, both of 1 Northumberland Fusiliers, were reported missing on 24 August and 26 August, respectively. Both were subsequently found to be prisoners of war. As can be expected, mistakes were made. Mrs Grogden, of 6 Duke Street, Millfield, was informed that her husband, in 1/Northumberland Fusiliers, was reported missing on 25 August. She subsequently heard from him on three separate occasions, each letter dated after the date of his purported capture.

Rifleman William Smith, Rifle Brigade, of 14 Chatterton Street, High Southwick, a recalled Reservist who had been a bricklayer at Wearmouth Colliery and a Boer War veteran, wrote home to say that he had received shrapnel wounds in his hand and foot during the retreat from Mons. His wounds had been dressed at St Quentin, at which place he was asked if he wanted to remain there, with the promise of capture. He refused and left with his regiment, being sent later to hospital at Rouen. He also made the comment that the German shrapnel was worse than their rifle fire.

Corporal Naylor, King's Royal Rifle Corps, wrote to his mother at 4 Cecil Street from his hospital bed in the Southern General Hospital, Birmingham, to tell her of his experiences at the front. At Mons he told her he had a near miss when a shell burst quite near him. He was leading his men along a road when the shell landed. He could feel the shrapnel whizzing past him; luckily he was not hit. Later during the battle he reported that the Germans had advanced in a solid mass, making a splendid target, and that his regiment had mowed them down. All attempts by the Germans to advance were brought to a halt. When the order to retire was received his men were furious but obeyed. Most of the wounds suffered by his men were from shrapnel, very few from rifle fire, which confirmed Rifleman Smith's comments.

The BEF was organized on a two-corps basis. During the retreat they encountered the Forest of Mormal, which was 9 miles long and a couple of miles wide. The British command, not having adequate maps of the area, made a decision to send one corps down each side of the forest, thus losing contact with one another. The Germans were able to make an assault on the town of Landrecies, taking the British I Corps initially by surprise. The battle was fought by the 4/Guards Brigade, which allowed the remainder of the corps to retire. Corporal J. Colquhoun, Coldstream Guards, who had served in 3/Volunteer Battalion Durham Light Infantry during the Boer War, took part in the action at Landrecies. He said that, initially, when the regiment was on its way to take up its position, it had been informed by a cavalry patrol that there were no Germans within miles of them. Shortly afterwards, the Germans came advancing down the road, taking the Guards by surprise. The Coldstreams took up position on the road, between two houses, with barbed wire from the farms on either side of them. This proved to be a very useful barrier against the German advance; some got partially over the wire before being shot. At one part of the action the German pressure was so great that the Coldstreams almost retired, but they were rallied by one of their officers, Major Matheson. Corporal Colquhoun stated that some of the Germans tried to gain an advantage by declaring themselves French. Any that tried to do so were shot. The Germans kept up the pressure until the early morning of 26 August, when the battle tailed off and the Guards Brigade took advantage of this to continue with their retirement.

It was not only in France that Sunderland men were being injured. At sea various patrols were maintained by the Admiralty, one such being made up of obsolete armoured cruisers. On 22 September, HMS *Aboukir*, HMS *Hogue* and HMS *Cressy* were on patrol

An artist's impression of the torpedoing and sinking of the three ships *Aboukir*, *Hogue* and *Cressy*.

HMS *Cressy,* sunk by the German submarine U9.

in the North Sea when they were sighted by the German submarine U9. HMS *Aboukir* was the first to be torpedoed. The other two ships stopped to pick up survivors, thinking that *Aboukir* had only hit a mine. When it was discovered that she had been torpedoed orders were given for the other two ships to get under way, but it was too late. HMS *Hogue* was the next to be hit, sinking within minutes. HMS *Cressy* managed to get under way but unfortunately was hit by two torpedoes, and she too sank. There was great loss of life. The ships' companies were made up mainly of Reservists. W. Wake, Royal Naval Reserve of 5 Dean Yard, Sunderland, who served in the Mercantile Marine prior to call-up, was a stoker serving on board HMS *Cressy* when she was hit. Luckily he survived the incident and was picked up by a Dutch fishing trawler. He landed at IJmuiden in the Netherlands, from where he wrote to his wife to say that he was safe and well and the Dutch were treating him well. In another letter he told his wife of his experiences that day. He had been standing amidships, helping with the rescue of the men from the other ships, when the torpedo hit, not far from where he was. The deck plates and woodwork went flying in the air, due to the explosion, and a great pillar of water erupted. Luckily he was not touched either by the explosion or by the falling wreckage. He waited until the situation had settled somewhat, then jumped into the sea and got clear of the ship. While in the water he found a mess table, which he was able to climb onto, being joined later by another sailor. It was during this time that he witnessed the captain going down with the ship, and a friend of his – William Lowery (thirty-nine), from 57 Burdon Street, Ryhope, also a stoker – go under. He was in the water for four and a half hours before being picked up.

Meanwhile in the Pacific, the SMS *Emden*, a German cruiser used as a commerce raider, sank three vessels that had been built by Sunderland shipbuilders Messrs J.L. Thompson and Sons. The ships were *King Lud* (sunk 25 September 1914), the *Riberia* (sunk 28 September 1914), and the *Foyle* (sunk 28/29 September 1914).

B.B. Frobisher, of Ivy House, Ellerslie Road, had first-hand experience of the SMS *Emden*. He was the chief engineer on the National Steamship Company of Greece ship

SMS *Emden*.

Pontoporos when she was captured by the *Emden* and forced to be in attendance to her. The *Pontoporos* was captured in the Bay of Bengal while carrying coal from Karachi to Calcutta. The *Emden* signalled her to stop and then put two shots over her bows. The *Pontoporos* was boarded by the Germans and Mr Frobisher spent two hours showing a German engineer the stokeholes and engines before he was transferred to the cruiser. When he came on board he was greeted by their chief engineer who said, 'Mr Chief, you will be treated like a gentleman. We can never tell but we may be prisoners next.' Later during his captivity Mr Frobisher was transferred to the *Markomanaria*, which was captured by HMS *Yarmouth*, thus enabling him to return home. HMS *Yarmouth* was also responsible for the recapture of the *Pontoporos*.

It was declared that the first wounded had arrived in Sunderland on 17 September, eleven in number, at the Eye Infirmary. They arrived at the railway station, in the charge of a nurse, and had to make their own way up the south incline to waiting transport. It was commented upon that there was no civic reception and that a more enthusiastic greeting could have been provided. At first it was believed the wounded had come from the front but on later investigation it turned out that all the cases were the results of sickness or accident.

While the men were away at the front the Salvation Army was helping to look after their dependants. Up until the middle of September, they had made 2,500 visits of an informal nature, for 320 of them using a motor car lent by Major Cuthbert Vaux. The Salvation Army helped with letters to the authorities concerning separation allowance etc. They also organized social meetings on Monday mornings for wives and mothers to keep in touch and discuss matters with each other. The Salvation Army Special Services Legion wrote letters to soldiers and sailors for those dependants who needed help with their literacy.

The soldiers serving in the area were also not forgotten by the Salvation Army. The Salvation Army Tramps, twenty in number, were volunteers who visited the local camps with gifts of cakes and other foodstuffs, plus a selection of literature. Quite often the Tramps were themselves entertained to tea in the officers' mess tent.

Concern was being raised about the level of alcohol consumption among the soldiers along the coast. The commander of the Tyne Defences issued an order prohibiting licence holders from serving soldiers in uniform except between 12.30 pm and 1.30 pm, and 6.00 pm and 8.00 pm in certain districts. Sunderland, which formed part of the Tyne Garrison, was included in the order.

Recruitment for the Durham Light Infantry Pals battalion (18/Durham Light Infantry) was disappointing. It was stated that by the end of September only fifty men from the town had joined up. Although the class of recruit was excellent, being from the professional and clerical classes, it was also thought that the battalion would be sent to the front before some of the Territorial Force battalions because its recruits would learn their skills more quickly. The battalion moved to Cocken Hall, near Newton Hall, Durham, to continue its training.

Other battalions were on the move. Sunderland recruits, serving in various units of Northern Command, were being sent to Frensham Common, near Farnham, Surrey.

Overall, recruitment in Sunderland was slowing down by the end of September, which was due partly to measurement standards being prohibitive and regiments open to receive new recruits being few in number. At the same time, a number of complaints had been received concerning the delays in paying separation allowances, which were leaving some families in a bad way. The Army quickly addressed the last complaint. A new form was introduced for each new recruit, on which he had to declare his wife and number of children. This form was completed on recruitment and all forms were sent each evening to the regimental paymaster to ensure prompt payment.

The Reverend Father James Stack left St Benet's, Monkwearmouth, to be chaplain to a Scottish regiment in September. St Benet's was in the area that suffered damage from the German Zeppelin raid in April 1916.

Again towards the end of September, those Germans and Austrians who had been arrested in the town and harbour were moved to a camp at York. All were sorry to leave Sunderland. On the afternoon of 3 October, Mrs Ahlers, her son, daughter, a gentleman friend and two maids were arrested at Sugley House, Roker, under the Defence of the Realm Act 1914. Mrs Ahlers was the wife of the German consul for Sunderland, who himself was awaiting trial at Durham Assizes.

Nicholans Emil Adolf Herman Ahlers (fifty), a naturalized Englishman and German consul for Sunderland, came to trial on 8 December 1914 on a charge of assisting German Reservists to leave England. The government placed quite a bit of importance to the case because the prosecution was led by the Solicitor General, Sir Stanley Owen Buckmaster. Mr Ahlers had been living in England for thirty years and had been the German consul in the town since 1905. At his trial, in his defence it was claimed that his duties as consul consisted of looking after the interests of the German Empire in relation to commerce, business and shipping and to protect and further the same assiduously, according to the laws of the

Nicholans Emil Adolf Herman Ahlers, German consul.

Houses overlooking Roker Beach, where Ahlers lived.

German state. One of these laws was that all German subjects of military age, between seventeen and forty-five, in case of war had to report for service. Mr Ahlers knew of war with Russia, France and Belgium, but not with England, the ultimatum not having expired. Also in his defence his council stated that under an Order in Council made under the Aliens Restriction Act 1914, it stated that subjects of the German Empire could leave the country between 4 and 11 August. The trial, which took place over two days, attracted much international press attention and on 9 December the defendant was found guilty and a sentence of death was passed, with a right of appeal being granted.

Ahler's appeal was heard before a specially constituted court of the Court of Criminal Appeal, on 18 December, when his conviction was quashed. His wife learned of the verdict while in Durham Prison, awaiting confirmation from the Home Office for her release.

It was during September/October that men of the Territorial Force were asked if they would serve overseas. The local battalion, 7/Durham Light Infantry, were at Scots House, on the road from East Boldon to Gateshead, when they were formed up in a hollow square. Private Joe Robson remembers:

> The Battalion marched to Scots House on the Newcastle Road. We were billeted in there. We were there for two or three days when Colonel Vaux, the Commanding Officer, came in on his horse, we were all lined up in the grounds. He asked for drafts to go to France, all the boys were quaking. Volunteers had to take three paces forward. I was one of them and they took our names.

Those men of the Territorial Force who volunteered were awarded a badge to wear on the right breast of their tunic, which said 'Imperial Service'. Private Stan Douglass recalled that for some men volunteering was not possible due either to personal reasons or that they were still at university. He also recalled that those who did not volunteer were made to march at the rear of the

Private Stanley Douglass, B Company, 7/Durham Light Infantry.

Imperial Service Badge, awarded to those who volunteered to serve overseas.

battalion when it returned to Sunderland and that the crowd booed them.

The town council received a letter from the Home Office regarding lighting. It was a letter addressed to all local authorities along the coast. The letter stated that lighting was either to be turned off or reduced. It had been proven by the Admiralty that the general glow from the town could be seen 25 miles out to sea. This glow would aid any German raider or submarine with its bearings. Although the lights on Sunderland's Esplanade had already been turned off, it was requested that skylights, illuminated fascias and powerful advertising also be turned off, or at least dimmed. It was emphasized that the Home Office had the power under an Order in Council, granted under the Defence of the Realm Act 1914, to order the lights to be extinguished or obscured.

Events in France were moving quickly. By September, the BEF was no longer in retreat but advancing, with the Germans falling back to prepared positions on the heights above the river Aisne. The Allies tried unsuccessfully to eject the Germans from this strong position. Tales started to come from the front regarding this battle. One such came from Private William Brodie, of 117 Battery Royal Field Artillery. He said that on 14 September his battery was shelling a factory when a German officer came out bearing a white flag and asked for a two-hour armistice in order to bury their dead and remove the wounded. This was agreed to. When hostilities commenced his battery was heavily shelled and were forced to retire, losing four killed and eight wounded. During the ceasefire the Germans had taken the opportunity to take the range of his battery. The battery's new position provided plenty of cover and it took the Germans five days before they found them. When they did, they brought down a heavy fire on them, killing one man, wounding eight others and knocking out two guns. Private Brodie was himself wounded on 23 September with shrapnel in his back.

It was also reported that P.C. Allan Hedley McLagan, of Barrington Street, had been killed on 14 September, while serving with 3/Coldstream Guards. He left a wife and one child. His father had died shortly before the news of the death of his son had arrived. It had previously been brought to his attention that his son had been severely wounded and it was thought that this had had an adverse affect on his health.

Also in 3/Coldstream Guards was Private Ronald Priest, who said that the battalion had pushed the Germans back over a rise but they had rallied and come back. This forced Private Priest to fall back with the rest of his section. However, during the retirement he was wounded in the right elbow and fell to the ground. The Germans left him but took the rations from his haversack. Private Priest lay out until dark, when he was able to return to his own lines.

Private J.T. Gallagher, B Company, 2/Durham Light Infantry, who resided at 33 Numbers Garth, Sunderland, wrote home to say that during the battle, at one time he and a friend called Frank were responsible for a frontage of 20 yards. The rest of the section had been either wounded or killed, the majority of them being Sunderland men. Later during the action, Private Gallagher was himself wounded. In his letter Private Gallagher mentioned that he had been 'bowled over' and people thought that this meant he had been killed. He had to explain that it was a common expression used by soldiers that meant 'wounded'.

The Sunderland Waifs' Rescue Agency and Street Vendors' Club received a letter from a former member, Fred Burlinson, who was serving in France as a despatch carrier between the cavalry and a field ambulance, to say that he was doing well. In all, sixty-three members of the Lambton Street Boys' Club had joined the Army and the Navy. Frederick Burlinson later transferred to the Royal Flying Corps and was unfortunately killed on 14 July 1917. He is buried in Vlamertinghe New Military Cemetery, Belgium.

Support for the Mayor's Local Relief Fund was growing. Not only were workers at the shipyards, coal mines and various factories voting to contribute a proportion of their wage but this was also happening in the world of entertainment. It was announced that during the week of 9 November, Mark Sheridan, a well-known and popular music hall singer and comedian who was to appear at the Sunderland Empire Theatre, had agreed to donate the whole of his salary, amounting to £175, to the fund. In addition to this the theatre itself was to donate the net profits, together with the entire proceeds of a special Wednesday matinee performance. It should be noted that collections for other funds had taken place in the theatre. Mr Edward John Everdell, the workhouse master, sent four shillings to the mayor to go towards the fund. The money had been collected by 'the old and infirm women'. The fund had caught a lot of people's imagination and urged them to contribute.

Mr W. Paul, a horse trader from Trimdon Street, presented a donkey to the chief constable for the local relief fund. The donkey, which was kept at the fire station, was to be put to use by the Boy Scouts when they collected funds in the town. He was given the name Teddy and it was later reported that he did sterling work, being extremely good for collecting. He was used for two weeks, taking his final bow at the Empire Theatre. Afterwards he was auctioned off.

An appeal from the ship's company of HMS *Hawke*, which was on patrol in the North

Sea, was received by the ladies of the Bede Tower Depot VAD for 650 helmets, belts, mufflers and mittens. This appeal for contributions was then made known to the people of the town. It is believed to be the first such appeal by the crew of a ship to a single town.

The imagined threat by German spies continued to play on the fears of the authorities; as a result, all owners of homing pigeons had to register with the police.

Towards the middle of October, recruitment in the town for 18/Durham Light Infantry ceased, the battalion being nearly up to strength. Recruitment continued only in Durham City. It was now suggested that the town seek approval from the War Office to raise a commercial battalion, similar to those of the Northumberland Fusiliers then being recruited. Although recruitment was generally satisfactory it was noted that from the commercial class it had been comparatively small.

Another home force being raised was the Civic Guard. The first meeting took place on 14 October at Westcott House. H. Pallister was elected chairman, J. Holmes treasurer, W.W. Seaton secretary, and a committee of fourteen were nominated and approved. Drill nights for the Guards would be on Monday and Wednesday evenings between 8.00 and 9.30 pm, and on Sunday afternoons, when drill would comprise route marches. All drill would be under the supervision of Chief Drill Instructor J.W. King. The Guards were given permission to use the grounds of Ford Estate, and Sunderland Rifle Club offered the use of their ranges. The committee of the Guards wanted to obtain early recognition from the War Office and it was therefore essential that the Guards did not interfere with recruitment for the Army and the Navy. Recruitment was open to all over the age of thirty-five. Those under that age who, due to family, business or private reasons, were unable to enlist, would have their applications to join considered by the committee. If the War Office specified that no one under thirty-five could join, those already in the Guards would be transferred to another corps.

Their first route march took place on 31 October, to Durham. The Guards, under the command of Captain King, were accompanied by the band of the Boy Scouts as far as Houghton-le-Spring. The march started at 9.30 am, with lunch at Raven Flat Farm, followed by some free time in Durham itself. The return march commenced at 3.00 pm, with the Boy Scouts' band rejoining at Houghton for the return parade through the town. About 130 men took part. This was followed shortly afterwards by their first drill night at High Barnes School, with Captain King taking the ex-servicemen, while the other Guards were under the instruction of Sergeant Cooke and Corporal Isherwood. Due to the large number of men on parade the town council gave their permission for the use of the school playing fields on Saturday and Sunday afternoons. Eventually, the Guards were formed into companies, at which time they were given use of the grounds of Ford Hall, where a rifle range had been constructed. It was proposed, in November, for a corps to be raised from the Guards to assist when necessary the military and the police. It was thought that 1,000 men would be wanted for this special duty.

While battles were raging in France, the Germans were continuing to march along the Belgian coast. By 5 October they were threatening Antwerp and it had been decided by the British Government to send three naval brigades to the city, which arrived on that date. Events were moving fast. The Germans started to bombard the city. The British forces were inadequate for the task set them. By 8 October, the naval brigades had begun to retire down the coast and Antwerp fell to the Germans on 10 October.

A man from Southwick who had been part of one of the naval brigades on his return to Sunderland told of his experiences. Prior to enlisting in Kitchener's Army he had worked in the pits in the area. While training, a call for volunteers to join the Royal Naval Division was made and he duly volunteered, together with hundreds of others. On being accepted he was sent to Eastry, which is near Sandwich, on the south coast. For the first month his training consisted of ordinary drill with occasional practices on the miniature range. Suddenly they were informed that they would be going abroad. He travelled to Dunkirk, via Dover, where he was put on a train for Antwerp. On arrival the brigades were billeted in schools and stables. He said that he spent most of the time digging trenches while under artillery fire. All of a sudden he and his comrades were told to leave the trenches and forget their kit … just get out. The streets of the city were crowded with refugees and the petroleum tanks on the waterside were ablaze. He and his comrades then commenced a night march of more than 30 miles, eventually arriving in Bruges, where a bread ration was issued. From there they entrained for Ostend, ending up back in Dover. One of his criticisms was the lack of British artillery to counter that of the Germans. He had been sent home for a couple of weeks before having to return to his unit on the south coast.

Another Sunderland man caught up in the situation at Antwerp was Nichol Martin of Martin & Co compass makers and maritime optics, who wrote of his experiences, from London, to his father, who resided at 39 Roker Baths Road. He was in the city on business when the Germans arrived. When the shelling started people moved to their cellars. Mr Martin went to some friends to whom he had promised shelter in the cellars of the house in which he was staying. Some of the houses in their street were already on fire and had to be left to burn themselves out as there was no water for the firemen. Having safely brought his friends back, he was advised, being an Englishman, to get out of the city. He caught a lighter for Flushing (Vlissingen), in the Netherlands. The boat was very full, with no food on board and the only water available was from the river. When the boat eventually got to Flushing he found it very crowded, but the Dutch people treated them very well.

Private Thomas Stoddart, Royal Marine Light Infantry, of 7 Bramwell Street, celebrated his eighteenth birthday in the trenches at Antwerp. He had joined the RMLI in June 1914. Private Stoddart landed at Antwerp at 4 o'clock in the morning and went straight into the trenches, where, he said, he simply sat down, under the occasional shell from the German artillery. Eventually the Germans found the range of the British trenches, which forced them to retire. Private Stoddart didn't see many Germans but heard them playing *God Save the King* and all the British bugle calls. He spent eighty hours in the trenches, without much food, before being pulled back to Ostend.

Back in Sunderland, the funeral, with full military honours, took place on 14 October of Private Samuel Coffey of the Royal Highlanders (Black Watch) at St Cuthbert's churchyard, West Herrington. Private Coffey, of 13 George Street West, New Herrington, left a wife, but had no children, and had worked at the local pits in the Herrington area. He had died in a Cambridge hospital from gunshot wounds received at Rheims. The Reverend

Parr took the service in the Church of St Aidan, New Herrington, before the interment. Crowds lined the route and 120 men from 2/Battery, 3/Northumberland (Reserve) Brigade RFA, under Lieutenant C.R. Common, escorted the coffin, and eight men of the battery acted as pallbearers.

The people of the town were anxious to play host to Belgian refugees and wounded soldiers. Around midnight on Friday, 16 October, thousands of the town's inhabitants congregated at the railway station to greet wounded soldiers. Unfortunately, the train was delayed and did not arrive until 6.34 am the next morning. But the crowd had waited. The police, together with 130 men of the York and Lancs Regiment, formed a cordon around the station. Union Street, from Holmeside to Athenaeum Street, was closed to the public. At the station were 200 St John Ambulance personnel, whilst outside were forty motors, lent by their owners, and fifteen horse ambulances. First off the train were the walking wounded, followed by those on stretchers. All were given a stamped postcard so that they could inform their relatives that they had arrived in Sunderland. When they made their appearance at the head of the platform, the crowd broke into cheers. There were seventy-four walking wounded and about twenty stretcher cases; all were taken to the infirmary. The crowd were informed that none of the wounded soldiers were Belgian. Later, the Wearmouth Colliery and surrounding districts divisions of the St John Ambulance thanked Mr Joe Andy, manager of the Queen's Kinema, for free admission to the picture hall during the unforeseen hours of waiting.

The grave of Private Samuel Coffey, St Cuthbert's Churchyard, West Herrington.

It was not until the end of October that the people of Sunderland got their wish to play host to wounded Belgian soldiers. On 29 October, forty wounded British and Belgian soldiers arrived in the town and were sent to Hammerton House and the Jeffrey Memorial Hall – Monkwearmouth VAD hospitals. The crowds on the station platform and in the booking hall broke into cheers at the sight of the men. Six Belgians – Emile Zoel, N. Burguell, Emile de Lange, Cyrille Lafeere, A. Lawrout and H. Davide – were sent to Hammerton House, whilst Claude Pauls (9 Belgian Infantry), Constant Blampair (a Lancer regiment) and Alfonso Von Heyste (Belgian Infantry) were part of the first complement of wounded to be sent to the Jeffrey Memorial Hall. Miss Aldis was Acting Lady Superintendent, assisted by two qualified nurses and aided by a staff of volunteer helpers connected with the VAD. The people of the town wanting to visit the wounded became so numerous that the routine of the hospital started to suffer; the wounded were becoming tired and the visitors spoiled the air of the wards. As a result, a routine of visiting hours was introduced – 2.00 pm until 4.00 pm – and the numbers of visitors were similarly restricted.

Something that caused controversy in the town was the decision to stop free rides on borough trams for soldiers, except those on military duty. This prompted letters to the local paper claiming that it was a disgrace. At this time, the town clerk received the following letter from the secretary to the Local Government Board:

Sir,

I am directed by the Local Government Board to state that they have been informed by the Home Office that it is now considered inadvisable to send aliens to towns and districts on the east and south-east coast. In the circumstances it is at present impossible to take advantage of hospitality which had been offered to Belgian refugees in those towns and districts.

Instructions were also issued for the arrest of all Germans, Austrians and Hungarians of military age. The North East coast was effectively to become a prohibited area for them.

Around the same time, the chief constable also received a letter from the Home Office that stated:

Any alien enemy residing in your area who has already changed his name since the outbreak of war should be warned to resume the name by which he was previously known, and if he does not do so within a reasonable time proceedings should be taken against him under Article 26 Aliens Restrictions (Consolidation) Order. As regards any future change of name proceedings should be taken as soon as it becomes known.

Sad news continued to arrive in the town. Mrs Thompson, of 5 John Street, Southwick, received her husband's identity disc and other personal effects from the War Office. Her husband, Walter Darcey Thompson, had been killed in action on 16 September while serving with 2/Coldstream Guards. He had been a Reservist, employed as a stoneman at Castletown Colliery before being recalled to the colours on the outbreak of war. On the very day of his death he had become entitled to a pension. Private Thompson was very keen on his football and during the 1912-13 season he was the secretary of the Southwick Football Club. He left a wife, who was seven months' pregnant, and two other children. The last entry in his diary was, '8.00 am Wednesday 16 September wet through we move on to a farm to get under cover.' It is believed that Private Thompson was the first soldier from Southwick to be killed in the war; he had seen action during the retreat from Mons, at the Battle of the Marne and on the Aisne. It is sad to relate that Mrs Thompson died in March 1915 and the three children were adopted by families in Southwick.

Word also came through of the death of Engine Room Artificer Class III, Joseph Stothard, from South Hylton, who was killed on 18 October while serving on the submarine E3. He was twenty-seven, had served six years in the Navy and was unmarried. The E3 has the distinction of being the first submarine to be sunk by another submarine, the U27, when she was torpedoed. All three officers and twenty-eight crewmen were lost on that day.

Another sailor from the town who had his ship sunk from under him was Petty Officer Class II Thomas Edwin Ost, of 59 Fowler Street. PO Ost was a Reservist, being an engineer at the docks before the war. He said that he was having breakfast when the torpedo struck. Everyone was ordered to their posts. The sick were taken off first, and then the order for abandon ship was given. Thomas Ost was in the water for half an hour, clinging to an empty petrol can before, being picked up.

It was towards the end of October that thoughts were beginning to turn towards Christmas. It was announced that an appeal was to be launched to raise funds to buy Christmas puddings for the wives and families of soldiers of the town who were on active service or had enlisted since the war had begun. Captain Smith of the Salvation Army, in Southwick, proposed a Christmas party for the children between the ages of six and fourteen of service personnel from Southwick. It was to comprise of a tea party with fruit, and a concert. If enough funds were raised, it was proposed that New Year's Day would be similarly celebrated. The management of the Savoy Hall gave the use of the hall free of charge to Captain Smith for the Christmas afternoon celebrations. Mr Noble, of the Gem Palace Picture House, held a collection every night for one week to raise funds for Captain Smith.

A report was circulated early in November to the effect that there had been between 17,000 and 18,000 men enlisted in the Sunderland area, which included South Shields, Jarrow, Darlington, Durham and all places in between. When the figures were analysed it showed that the number of recruits from the town itself was only about 2,000; this figure was lower than those for South Shields and Durham. In addition to that, eighty per cent were married men; therefore, a call went out for single men to do their bit. Recruiting for the Tyneside Irish Battalion was proceeding well, with a recruiting meeting being held at St Peter's, Green Street, when it was hoped that the Irish men of the town would enlist. Councillor Hoey was the recruiting officer for the battalion in the town, with an office at 204 High Street West, which had been decked out in patriotic flags and bunting.

One day in November, rumours began circulating around the town that an enemy mine-laying vessel was being escorted into Sunderland Harbour by two torpedo boats. This turned out to be untrue. The true story was that the Dutch vessel *Wieringen*, laden with grain and on its way to Sunderland, had been escorted across the North Sea by the two torpedo boats.

Thoughts of those left behind were continually in the minds of people in the town. Workmen of the Sunderland Shipbuilders Co. yard clubbed together for a collection for the widows of James Watson and Robert Sandilands, co-workers who had been killed. Each widow received £19 5s. Both soldiers had been killed in action on 21 September while serving with 2/Durham Light Infantry.

A letter from a major in France was sent to the *Sunderland Echo* saying that the men of the Sunderland Heavy Battery had been attached to 116/Heavy Battery and were getting on well with the conditions and their duties. There had been some wounded, at times severely. It was stated that the men had been in action continually for thirteen days and one afternoon, while under heavy fire, and the order came to withdraw the guns. The Sunderland drivers kept their heads down and just got on with the job; the guns were safely got away.

One of those unfortunate and ironic incidents that happen in times of war occurred on 11 November. Private John Smith, 3/York and Lancs Regiment, did not heed the warnings of a sentry, who aimed his rifle at him and pulled the trigger. Private Smith was hit in the head and killed. The sentry was arrested but claimed that he did not realize the rifle was loaded. Private Smith was buried, with full military honours, in Mere Knolls Cemetery, Sunderland. The firing party led the procession, and then came the band, playing the *Dead March* from Handel's *Saul*, followed by the hearse, and then 150 men of his regiment under the command of Captain Thompson.

In the town there were the beginnings of fierce rivalry with other parts of the country – nowhere more so than in the areas of recruiting and fundraising – which carried on throughout the war. On 14 November, a collection was undertaken for the orphan children of Belgian soldiers and it was hoped at the beginning to raise more than Middlesbrough and Darlington. The collection was done by the 'lady school teachers and scholars', comprising 1,400 in total, assisted by the Girl Guides and Boy Scouts. During the afternoon a collection was taken at Roker Park Football Ground, each contributor receiving a Belgian flag brooch. The collection was under the patronage of the mayoress, Mrs Richardson, and HRH the Duchess of Vendome, a sister of the Belgian king. In total, £900 was raised, but from this had to be deducted the costs of the flags, adverts, etc.

Ways to improve the numbers of men joining the colours were constantly being devised by the government, with instructions issued to local recruiting officers. Major Byrne received the following letter about a new enlistment scheme:

I am directed to inform you that the Parliamentary Recruiting Committee have for some time under consideration a scheme to assist the Military Recruiting Authorities to obtain men for enlistment in the army for the period of the war. The following is an outline of the scheme it is proposed shortly to put into force in each of the recruiting areas. The Parliamentary Committee will (1) by means of forms endeavour to obtain the names of all men willing to serve for the period of the war; (2) issue and distribute suitable publications in leaflet and pamphlet form; (3) Parliamentary speakers to hold public meetings; and (4) assist the recruiting authorities and their agents with regard to (1). The forms will be issued to householders who will be asked to fill them up and return them to 12 Downing Street, London. The forms will there be sorted and will be sent to the recruiting area commander concerned. It is particularly desired that on receipt of these forms the area commander shall have rolls made out from them of all men willing to enlist and that they shall call up the men as fast as they can deal with them.

All recruiting officers are to be most careful to explain to any men who are not up to the standard in force at the time why they cannot be accepted at the moment, and also make it quite clear to them that they will be again called up should the standard be altered so as to include them.

In cases where men are rejected on medical grounds, recruiting officers should treat them with the greatest tact and consideration and should invite their assistance to get further recruits from those who have not yet stated that they are willing to serve.

The men who are willing to serve for the period of the war will receive a certificate of registration in which are contained spaces for recording the names and address of the recruit, the date of his registration, his age and the medical officer's remarks.

This letter came at a time when recruiting from Sunderland was a cause for concern. Major Byrne had said that recruiting in the town was 'wretched and very much worse than South Shields, where there are fewer eligible men'. The major published figures of the men serving in the Army from the town for the period 5 August to 19 October. The total figure was 6,520, of which 3,720 were new recruits, approximately 1,200 Army Reservists, 900 Special Reservists and approximately 700 Territorials. Sunderland District had been honoured, by invitation, to raise a company for the Inniskilling Fusiliers, to be designated the Wearside Company. The NCOs were to be selected from amongst the company.

At this time the standards for recruiting were strictly adhered to. For instance, men had to be over 5 feet 3 inches, with a minimum chest measurement of 34 inches. This restriction prohibited a large number of men from enlisting. It was therefore decided to create a bantam battalion, known as the Birkenhead Bantam Battalion, comprising men in height from 5 feet to 5 feet 3 inches, as so many had come forward wanting to serve. The leading character in the raising of the first bantam battalion was Alfred Bigland, the Member of Parliament for Birkenhead, who wrote to Lord Kitchener proposing the idea. After receiving the go-ahead he informed every recruiting office in the country to accept men for the battalion. It was stated that these men should be of a 'square sturdy build', and soon the district sent sixty men to the battalion, mainly from the colliery area, with recruiting closing after only a few days. The battalion was designated 15 (Service) Battalion (First Birkenhead), The Cheshire Regiment. It was hoped, soon afterwards, to raise a bantam battalion from the Durham area alone, but approval for this did not come until January 1915. This battalion eventually became 19/Durham Light Infantry.

The War Office intimated that men with certain industrial training were required for the Army Ordnance Corps. The men required were blacksmiths, clerks, foremen, assistant foremen, hammermen, saddlers, storemen, tent makers and wheelers. Special appeals were issued by the War Office for recruits for particular units. One such was for carpenters, tailors and shoemakers, who would be given ordinary rates of pay and for shoesmiths and saddlers at five shillings a day for the Royal Engineers. Another appeal was for dockers, for transport work for three special sections of the Army Service Corps (Labour Company). The latter appeal involved Major Byrne obtaining permission of the authorities to raise the men from stevedores at the docks. He was required to find three foremen, to be given the rank of sergeant, at five shillings a day, six gangers at the rank of corporal, at four shillings a day, and 150 labourers to be given the rank of private, at three shilling a day.

A major recruiting meeting was held on 4 December at the Victoria Hall. The meeting was preceded by a musical programme, with wounded soldiers in attendance in the front rows. The assembly was addressed by Lord Charles Beresford, Member of Parliament for Sunderland. Lord Charles talked about the war, the need for men now to be trained, how the war was affecting everyone, of American public opinion and the valuable role of the Navy. His speech was well received by all. The next day there was a full dress parade, commanded by Brigadier General Pink, followed by a march through the town. It started at Roker Avenue, progressed to the High Street and along Hylton Road to Kayll

Road, returning to the town by Chester Road and ending in Stockton Road, with speeches in West Park. The parade was led by the East End Prize Band.

The recruiting offices were open all through December, closing only on Christmas Day, such was the need for recruits. Towards the end of December an advertisement was made to the men of the district to raise a Wearside company of the Tyneside Scottish. The offices would be at Maritime Building, which would be used for the preparation of advertisements, whilst the recruiting offices would be in John Street and Bridge Street. During a recruitment meeting at the Victoria Hall it was stated that the authorities needed men from the ages of nineteen to forty-five.

It was not only the military that was advertising for men. An appeal from William Doxford & Sons Limited, shipbuilders, was made to the shipbuilding, engineering, boiler building, brass foundry, plumbing and tinsmith workers of the town. The shipyard was to be run both day and night, including Sundays, for the construction of naval vessels. The appeal asked for all Sunderland men who had been drafted to other districts to return to work there for the honour and benefit of their own town. Those people already employed at the yard would assist in attaining their targets and show that the Wear could do as well as other districts in quality and despatch. All workers would be supplied by the Admiralty with certificates and badges showing the bearer to be employed on National Service. Prior to the war, Sunderland shipyards did very little for the Admiralty. As the week progressed, the call for shipyard workers intensified, with the phrase that they could 'hit as hard with the hammer and rivet as with rifle and bullet'.

A letter from a recruit in the town appeared in the *Sunderland Echo* encouraging others to enlist and telling of his daily routine. He got up at 06.30 am, with breakfast at 07.30 or 08.00 am, parade at 09.00 until lunch at 12.00, then parade from 2.00 pm until 4.00 pm. On Saturdays, morning parade took place as usual, with a finish at noon. He went on to say that he and his mates were allowed out every night after 4.30 pm and at weekends after 2.30 pm. He was given good meat and plenty of it to eat.

Restrictions continued to be applied in the town, especially at the sea front. An order under the Defence of the Realm Regulations 1914, by Brigadier General Francis J. Pink, the commander at Sunderland, required that, 'Whitburn Road between the north end of Roker Terrace, Sunderland and Whitburn Village to be closed to all pedestrian and vehicle traffic, both by day and by night, except trade-men's carts and people living in the road, who must be provided with passes signed by the Chief Officer of Police of the district in which they reside.' A request was also made for the Bede Memorial, which had been erected in 1904, to be removed from Cliff Park, and this was duly carried out. It was not replaced until 1921.

With all the men in uniform throughout the country there were bound to be frauds. Two such occurred in the town in early December. Corporal Frederick Bostock, Northumberland Fusiliers, and Lance Corporal Arthur Rose (regiment unknown) both posed as wounded soldiers, travelling around the town and obtaining food from charitable sources. While at the Seaman's Mission one Sunday evening, they were befriended by Mr Leadbitter, a chemist, who became interested in their plight. He entertained them at his home for a couple of days, feeding them and giving them free lodgings. After a few days he became suspicious and informed the police. The pair were taken to Major Byrne, who had them examined by a doctor, who found no wounds, although one wore an eye patch with the bridge of his nose being heavily bandaged, whilst the other had an arm in a sling. Both were subsequently arrested and remanded in custody.

One of the town's sporting personalities, Dennis Hendren, the Sunderland and Durham County Cricket Club's professional, joined the 18/Durham Light Infantry. Sunderland Cricket Club met with him and agreed to pay him a weekly salary until his return as the club professional. He had started his career in cricket in 1905 playing for Middlesex before coming north in 1910.

December saw another incident of window breaking in the town. John Rush, of the 7/Yorkshire Regiment, was arrested on two charges of wilful damage. First he broke the plate-glass windows at the eating house of Gustav Adolphus Theodore Strunk, of 9 High Street East. The second charge related to breaking the plate-glass window of Gustav William Hanselmann, pork butcher, of 243 High Street West. Mr Strunk said that at 6.10 pm on Saturday, 19 December, both he and his wife were in the shop when he saw a half brick come through the window. He went out into the street, where he saw Rush, who threw the other half brick at him. In respect to the second charge, Rush threw three missiles through the window. When he was apprehended a crowd tried to secure his release. In his defence Rush said that he could not remember anything about the incidents as he was drunk. Rush was committed for trial at the sessions.

Further south, on the morning of 16 December, three German ships, the battlecruisers *Moltke* and *Seydlitz*, together with the cruiser *Blücher*, shelled Hartlepool, and the battlecruisers *Derfflinger* and *Von der Tann* attacked Scarborough and Whitby. A great deal of damage was done to Hartlepool, resulting in more than 100 men, women and children being killed and approximately 300 more people wounded. Among the casualties were five men of the 18/Durham Light Infantry killed and eleven wounded. About eighteen people were killed in Scarborough. If Hartlepool, Scarborough and other coastal towns could be attacked, then so could others, including Sunderland. This whole incident sent shockwaves through the country. Questions were asked of the Royal Navy as to why it could not protect our own coast. A few days after the attack the Mayor of Sunderland made it known to the town that the fullest possible arrangements had been made by the Local Emergency Committee and there was therefore no cause for alarm. The military authorities had made full preparations for the defence of the town in the 'unlikely event of an attack'. He also said that the special constables would be issued

Fort built c1870 to guard the mouth of the river Wear. By 1914 it had become obsolete and did not possess any guns.

Site of the Roker Battery looking south, which was armed with two 4.7 naval guns.

Site of the Roker Battery looking north, 1915.

with full instructions for the direction of the general public. People were urged to keep indoors in the event of a bombardment and to remain on the floor and to use the basement, if they had one. Children would remain in school under the supervision of their teachers if an attack occurred during school hours, and parents were told not to collect them from school until the attack was over. At the time the only defence the town had was the Wave Basin Battery, which had been built during the 1870s, but due to the expansion of the port it was soon obsolete and no armaments were listed in the 1913 return. There had been another battery at Roker, built during the eighteenth century, but by 1902 the guns had been removed. However, two 4.7-inch naval guns were positioned there from February 1916. Another battery, known as the Abbs Battery, was constructed slightly to the north of the Roker Battery during the war and had two 4.7-inch quick-firing MkIV guns.

The people of the town were determined to celebrate Christmas Day as normal, although it would be tinged with sadness. In the run-up to Christmas the shops in the town were decorated and they displayed a wide range of gifts. On the day itself the inmates of the various public local institutions were entertained. The picture houses and music halls held a Christmas night programme, the usual carnival was held on the Garrison Field and toys and gifts were given to the children in hospital. However, it was business as usual the next day.

As already mentioned, trenches had been dug along the cliffs and sea front as part of the anti-invasion defences. Shortly after Christmas an unfortunate incident took place. Eleven-year-old Winifred Harle Summerside, of 83 Dock Street East, Monkwearmouth, was playing with other children when she fell into a trench at Sea View. Although the trench was only 3 feet 6 inches deep, her injuries were enough for her to be taken to Doctor Cox's surgery, where unfortunately she was pronounced dead on arrival, the cause of death being given as syncope (a drop in blood pressure). It was thought that if she had been left in the trench to recover she would have survived.

So ended the year 1914 for the town.

Chapter Two

1915: The year of innocence
Recruiting, rationing and requisitioning

THE NEW YEAR brought no let-up in the drive for recruits for the armed forces. On Friday, 22 January, a meeting of the Sunderland Recruiting Committee met to discuss the communication from Lord Kitchener that the mayor (Alderman S. Richardson) had received concerning the formation of a Wearside brigade of the Royal Field Artillery (RFA). The mayor had asked the committee to consider the matters raised by Lord Kitchener. Because there would be expense involved locally, the Chamber of Commerce was approached with a view to helping with the financial guarantee required by the War Office. The Chamber of Commerce, in turn, decided to ask the mayor to call a town meeting to consider the advisability of raising the unit. The mayor declined to hold a town meeting and asked both the Recruiting Committee and the Chamber of Commerce to deal with the matter. The invitation to raise a local unit was coldly received by the Chamber of Commerce, who thought that local recruiting was nearly exhausted. They stated that Sunderland and district had sent thousands of recruits to units throughout the country and that 11,000 men had already joined the Artillery. In view of the attitude at the time and that 800 men were willing to serve in the unit, the Recruiting Committee decided to proceed.

Consequently, on 5 February, the mayor replied to the War Office to inform them that the town would like to accept the invitation to raise a gun brigade consisting of a headquarters, four batteries, ammunition column (718 men in total) and first reinforcement (seventy-three men and one officer). At the same time, the mayor took the opportunity of nominating Colonel Charles William Panton Barker as its commanding officer. The War Office was quick to reply, thanking the mayor and asking him to liaise with the General Officer, Commander in Chief, Northern Command, regarding the raising and training of the brigade. Colonel Barker went on to become a Commander of the Civil Division of the Most Excellent Order of the British Empire for his war services in Sunderland. Sadly, his son, a major in the Royal Garrison Artillery, died in 1918 and has no known grave.

The local Recruiting Committee now became responsible for billeting, feeding, clothing, equipping and training the brigade, until the War Office could take over, which would take three to four months. This meant that the committee also had to make contracts and pay all accounts for the brigade, although the War Office would refund amounts expended monthly on submission of receipted accounts. There were certain costs that the committee would not be able to claim back, such as advertising and the difference between the Army allowance for clothing and the price at which the contracts were arranged. It was expected that this sum would not exceed £500. It was advertised that those men wishing to join the brigade could register their interest at any recruiting office or by sending a postcard to Mr J.A. Raine, Maritime Building, Sunderland. The committee was looking for: 402 gunners between 5 feet 7 inches and 5 feet 10 inches, 306 drivers between 5 feet 3 inches and 5 feet 7 inches, twenty-one farriers and shoeing smiths, ten saddlers, twelve sitters and wheelers and five storemen.

A meeting held on 12 February was opened by the mayor, where he said that he proposed to leave the matter of the raising of the brigade to the Recruiting Committee and that he had every confidence in them to do the job. He also made it known that Sunderland was mainly supporting two funds – the Prince of Wales Fund and the Mayor's Local Fund – besides the Belgian and other funds. Up to that date a total of £25,000 had been raised for the two funds, with a further £5,000 for the Belgian fund. In addition to this the town had sent two motor ambulances to the front, which were providing sterling service. Mr William Milburn, General Chairman of the Committee, was the next to speak. He said that £5,850 had already been promised, and £40 10s donated, towards the £10,000 required by the War Office for the finance guarantee and that an appeal was to be made shortly. He also informed the audience that of all the units raised throughout the country, none had 'Wearside' attached to their name and he felt that the town could find the men required. Already the town had supplied nearly 1,000 men to the Tyneside Irish and about 700, in three weeks, to the Tyneside Scottish. He felt that Sunderland was particularly an artillery district. Brigadier Kelly, Commander of the District, was the next to take the floor. He spoke of the types of men required. One type would have to be powerful men for managing the guns, having good sight and high intelligence, whilst the other would be lighter, more active men for driving horses (being animal lovers) and taking guns into position. The officers would have a great deal of responsibility and very difficult duties. The four batteries, each of four guns, would be commanded by a major, who would be in full charge and control of the firing done by the battery.

In sixteen days nearly 500 men had joined the brigade. All the drivers' vacancies had been filled, which left 180 gunners required. Training started at Houghton-le-Spring, with Houghton Hall, Kepier Grammar School and other premises being requisitioned. The hall provided the accommodation for the headquarters personnel and sleeping quarters for A Battery. There was a large recreation room and field of two or three acres where training and drill could be carried out. B Battery was billeted in the drill hall, C Battery was at the Primitive Methodist and Presbyterian school rooms and D Battery was in Kepier School. The War Office had accepted the mayor's suggestion and appointed Colonel Barker as commanding officer, with Captain Brandis, who had seen action in France, as adjutant. Houghton-Le-Spring welcomed the men of the brigade. The meals provided were of a good standard and quality; they were cooked on gas stoves and served in a large marquee. Initially the men had no uniforms, as these were in short supply due to the number of men joining the Army, and the training initially consisted of drill and route marches. The War Office had promised that guns would be supplied quickly.

On 20 May, the officers and men of 160 (Wearside) Brigade RFA marched to the town from their training camp at Houghton-le-Spring. The march started at 10.45 am and was met at the children's hospital by the band of 3/York and Lancs Regiment. At the town hall they were met by the mayor and other civic dignitaries, where the men saluted

Town Hall, with the railway station on the left.

the mayor on their march past. The parade continued on to the drill hall, the route lined with spectators. At the drill hall the mayor welcomed the men to the town and congratulated them on their smartness. The mayor provided the men with refreshments and a supply of cigarettes, while the officers were entertained to lunch at the Grand Hotel by the Recruiting Committee.

News was also released of the death of Private John Tindall, 2/Coldstream Guards, who died of his wounds on 5 February 1915. Private Tindall, who was twenty-six, was a member of the Borough Police Force, attached to Hendon District, before being recalled to the colours on the outbreak of the war. He lived with his mother at 6 Hume Street, Millfield, and now lies buried in Cuinchy Communal Cemetery, France.

Tragedy struck on 14 February at Roker Pier when Private John Thomas Thorp, 3/York & Lancs Regiment, was drowned as the result of an accident. He is buried in Mere Knolls Cemetery, Sunderland.

The effects of the war were starting to be felt at home. By January, food prices had risen substantially; butter was now being sold for 1s 6d, which was the highest price in thirty-five years. The price of bacon had also risen on account of the killing of smaller pigs in Denmark as a result of feed shortages, again caused by the pressures of the war. Cheese was in short supply due to the government buying most of the stock available. The increase in freight prices was not wholly responsible; there was congestion at the docks due to labour shortages, with men joining the forces. In addition to this there was a lack of light craft, as many of those available had been requisitioned by the government. At a meeting on 15 February, held at St Peter's Hall, Green Street, at which Mr F.W. Gladstone (Labour), MP for the Borough, was the principal speaker, Councillor Baxter moved the following resolution, which was passed:

> That this meeting protests against inactivity of the government in the matter of the high cost of commodities to the working classes of this country and calls upon the government forthwith to undertake the purchase, carriage and distribution at fair prices of food and fuel in order that the present burdens may as soon as possible be removed.

Mr Gladstone told the audience that it was no fault of the miners, as had been commonly thought, but that coal was eleven shillings a ton at the pit but fifty shillings a ton in the East End of London.

Since the start of the war various bodies had sprung up to help with the defence of the country and to provide an element of military training for men over the age of thirty-eight, as well as for those of military age who for one reason or another could not join the colours. By April 1915, the government was starting to organize nationally the various corps into the Volunteer Training Corps (VTC), the first battalion of which was affiliated in Sunderland in November 1914. The Athletes Unit had, by April 1915, wound up, although it had a large number of recruits.

During the winter of 1914/15, the VTC had accomplished a complete course in infantry and rifle drill. This battalion was mainly officered by shipyard and workshop managers and professional men. The shipyard of William Pickersgill Junior had more than 100 men in training at this time. Likewise, Messrs Swan and Hunter's had a platoon and the Scotia Engineering Works had more than 100 men enrolled. There had only been a small response from men in offices and banks, and a poor response from schoolmasters. A junior division of the VTC was formed comprising boys above the age of Boy Scouts but below that for enrolling in Kitchener's Army. Mr Samuel Storey, who was an ex-Member of Parliament for Sunderland in the 1880s and an ex-member of Durham County Council, was asked by the battalion to become the honorary commander, which he accepted, and the organization was put on a more regular footing.

The VTC, or Home Guard or Civil Guard, as it had been also known, was started by Sir Arthur Conan Doyle shortly after the commencement of the war and quickly spread throughout the country. Official recognition was at first withheld, but when the Central Association was formed under the presidency of Lord Desborough, and with General Sir O'Moore Creagh as military adviser, the War Office handed over responsibility for local defence forces to the association. There were certain conditions, however. One that created controversy was that men who were thirty-eight or below had to provide a reasonable excuse for not joining Kitchener's Army and to undertake to enlist if specifically called upon in a national emergency. Many men refused, feeling they may be tricked into going abroad. It was decided by the Under Secretary of State that those who refused to sign must leave the VTC. The reason for this rule was to prevent men shirking their duty of joining Kitchener's Army and saying that they were doing their bit by being a member of the VTC. Another condition was that the corps was to be uniformed at the expense of the corps itself, or the local community, and must not be attired in wool or khaki. As to military titles, there were to be no generals or colonels. With regard to arms, the Regular forces and Territorials had first claim.

The aims of the VTC were to encourage recruits for the Regular and Territorial Army and also to give men not of military age or otherwise disqualified for service, drill and instruction in the basics of musketry in their spare time and to co-ordinate existing organizations with similar bodies and promote uniformity in their rules and regulations. It was felt that many men would be prepared to help defend their country in a national emergency, such as invasion. It was thought that men with no military knowledge would take a long time to fit themselves for the emergency, but building on the modified training proposed, they would quickly become efficient soldiers.

During April, the 7/Durham Light Infantry, together with the rest of 50 Division, embarked for France, the advance party of three officers and eighty-six men leaving on 17 April and the main body on 19 April. Private Douglass remembered:

We embarked for France on 19 April 1915, they didn't tell you that, not in our language. We were only soldiers, we were all shoved onto a big troopship. There were a couple of Destroyers that we could see, we were all in the hold. The whole Battalion was on one troopship. It was one of the Liners that they used for holidays because all the fancy work was boarded off with wood so that we could not damage it with our rifles and things. We got over to Boulogne, we went up to a place called St Michaels Mount [Mont Saint-Michel] and we slept there overnight.

When they landed in France, the arrival and training of the battalion did not go as planned. After spending a night at Boulogne, they were moved up to the front, towards Ypres, in Belgium. On 22 April, the Germans launched a surprise gas attack at Ypres, which caused the French 87 (Territorial) and 45 (Algerian) divisions to retreat in disorder, thus leaving a gap in the line. To their right stood the Canadian Division, who, although forced to retire, managed to slow the Germans down. As a result reinforcements were rushed to the front. This included the 50 Division. Six days after arriving in France the 7/Durham Light Infantry were in action. Private Douglass, B Company, took part in this action, recalling:

We advanced, lay down, advanced again, fall down. Nobody knew what we were doing mind, it had not been explained. The third time we lay down the order came along 'Fix Bayonets'. Nothing happened before that but as soon as them bayonets went on all Hell broke out. He tossed everything at us. No rifle fire mind, just shellfire. The first experience I saw of it I took to be rags flying through the air, they were men really.

The battalion did not reach the German trenches; the attack was a feint. During the night they were recalled to their starting positions. Private Frank Surtees, A Company, who also took part in the advance, remembered:

There was the Colonel [Vaux] right at the head. He was standing with his shepherd's crook. There he was standing. I thought 'Look at that, there he is and they are pelting shells all over the show.' But he came out alright. He never budged. I looked out again as soon as one had gone off, I had a quick look up again, he's still there, he never got wounded.

Private Frank Surtees, A Company, 7/Durham Light Infantry.

Private Stanley Douglass in fighting order, having returned straight from the trenches in late 1916.

The Germans were firing all night, it was buzzing over your head and you just lay on your pack waiting for the daylight. It must have been about 2 o'clock in the morning, maybe later, all of a sudden, when it was dead quiet, the Colonel came past, he knew where we were lying. 'Come on lads, you've got to get the Hell out of this as quick as possible or you'll be blown to bits in the morning. Hurry up and fall in on the road, not in fours or twos but single file. Get away back where you come from.'

It was quite true because we had no trenches; we were on the top just behind the support.

The big trial for the battalion came on Whit Monday, 24 May, when A and B companies were attached to 3/Royal Fusiliers at Bellewaarde Ridge, north-east of Ypres. The Germans launched their final gas attack of what became known as the Second Battle of Ypres. Both companies suffered heavily. Private Douglass was one of those gassed:

On the Whit Monday of 1915 the gas attack started. We didn't know what it was. All we knew that morning was that it was a nice calm day with a breeze. We saw this smoky stuff coming over. Just before that Lieut Stockdale on my left, Brodie, my mate, was on the left of him. Stockdale dropped in the trench with a bullet right through his head. Rifle fire started to break out all over and still we didn't know it was gas. Then everybody started to cough and retch and retch and that's what happened to me. I got a sniff of it and I was retching and retching. All that I can remember is I saw the Germans coming, we had no gas masks, they were just like monsters to us because they had big snouts. It was a gas mask, just like a pig's snout. And all I remember is one of them bending over me; in fact he pulled me up and dropped me down again. And I was still retching and retching and groaning and I must have passed out. I don't know how I got out of the trench, but when I came too I was lying in Wipers [Ypres] Square, waiting for an ambulance to take me down to the Canadian Hospital.

Painting of *The Miracle of Ypres*, when the German gas was alleged to have gone over the Durhams when they sang hymns in May 1915.

2438 Private William Allan, 7/Durham Light Infantry, killed in action 24 May 1915 in France.

The Nairn brothers, from Southwick.

During the two days of intense action the battalion lost four officers killed, two missing and one wounded, with twenty-five other ranks killed, seventy-five wounded and 181 missing.

A number of families had all their sons, and sometimes husbands, serving in the forces. One such family was the Nairns, from Southwick. Mrs Nairn, a widow, had five sons and two daughters. All of her sons were in the forces, as was her son-in-law. John, Walter and William all served as buglers in 7/Durham Light Infantry (Walter died of wounds on 22 June 1915), George served in the cavalry and Henry in the Royal Army Medical Corps. She received a letter of thanks from the Keeper of the Privy Purse, on behalf of the king, for her family's contribution to the war effort.

In May, an incident took place that nearly brought the United States into the war. Earlier in February the Germans had declared the waters around the United Kingdom a war zone and had stated that any ship in those waters, regardless of flag, would be sunk without warning. So it was, on 7 May, that the *Lusitania* was torpedoed off the south-west coast of Ireland. The Germans had taken out adverts in American newspapers, prior to her sailing, to warn passengers of the danger. A total of 1,198 men, women and children lost their lives, including 124 American citizens.

One man aboard who survived to tell his tale was George Harrison, of 8 Thompson Terrace, Ryhope. He had been returning from Coal Creek, Canada, in order to join the Army. He had twice during the emergency voluntarily given up his life jacket to a young married woman with a child but was able to obtain one for himself from the First Class lounge. On his return to the deck he noticed a 'foreign gentleman' with no fewer than five life jackets who burst into tears when someone took one from him. When he had regained the deck he was witness to the launching of the first lifeboat but, unfortunately, due to the listing of the ship, the lifeboat was wrecked. The second lifeboat to be launched suffered the same fate. Mr Harrison dived into the water. When regaining the surface he witnessed the end of the liner, whose stern had partly lifted out of the water and a few seconds later slid beneath the waves. While in the water he was able to grab some wood, which he held on to, at the same time grabbing a young Irish girl who was floating past. Another young fellow joined him. Eventually they made their way to an upturned boat that had forty-eight people clinging to it. They were the last to join it. It was a further two hours before they were rescued. There were dead bodies and wreckage floating all over the area.

On the other side, Richard Leo Bryson, of Sunderland, who was a third officer in the Mercantile Marine, was on one of the ships that came to the rescue of the survivors. America protested vigorously to the Germans, who apologized and halted unrestricted U-boat warfare for the time being. America would not enter the war for another two years.

The Recruiting Committee for Sunderland and district had been under continual pressure since the commencement of hostilities to raise and, in some cases, equip and train men. In June, further pressure was brought to bear when they were asked by the War Office to raise an additional infantry battalion. After due deliberation the mayor and committee agreed and official authorization was sanctioned on 17 July. The new battalion would be named 20 (Service) Battalion Durham Light Infantry (Wearside), with Major K.J.W. Leather appointed to the command. Recruiting started on 19 August and it was emphasized that men could enlist together and serve in the same company or platoon together for training. It was planned to raise 1,350 men, 250 forming a depot company, and 250 later, when the battalion left for overseas. Those men joining on 19 August were given leave and told to report back on 23 August. The battalion were allocated billets at St John's Wesleyan School, Sunderland, with drilling on Ashbrooke Cricket Ground. Shortly afterwards, on 28 August, the battalion paraded at the school, 135-strong, and marched to Pallion Station to entrain for Wensley Camp, Wensleydale, headed by the band of 3/Durham Light Infantry, by way of the town hall, where the mayor wished them well.

The Victoria Cross is Britain's highest award for gallantry in the face of the enemy and since its creation in 1856, less than 1,400 have been awarded. It was announced in *The London Gazette* of 18 November 1915 that Captain George Allan Maling, Royal Army Medical Corps, attached to 12/Rifle Brigade, had won the coveted medal during the Battle of Loos for:

> The most conspicuous bravery and devotion to duty during the heavy fighting near Fauquissart on 25 September 1915. Lieutenant Maling worked incessantly with untiring energy from 6.15 am on the 25th till 8.00 am on the 26th, collecting and treating in the open under heavy shell fire more than 300 men. At about 11.00 am on the 25th he was flung down and temporarily stunned by the bursting of a large high-explosive shell, which wounded his only assistant and killed several of his patients. A second shell soon after covered him and his instruments with debris, but his high courage and zeal never failed him, and he continued his gallant work single-handed.

George Allan Maling was born in Sunderland on 6 October 1888, graduating as a doctor of medicine in 1914 from the University of Oxford and St Thomas's Hospital. Captain Maling was also mentioned in dispatches. He served for a period at the Military Hospital, Grantham, and then returned to France, serving with 34/Field Ambulance, 11 Division. He died on 9 July 1929, leaving a wife and one son, and is buried in Chislehurst Cemetery.

Captain George Allan Maling VC, RAMC.

On 6 December, the Dutch schooner *Geziena* ran ashore on the Beacon Rocks. The steel schooner was carrying a cargo of pit props from Norway to Hartlepool when it happened. The Sunderland Volunteer Life Brigade, together with the coastguard and soldiers stationed at the docks, went to her assistance. It was not possible to refloat the ship due to the shallow water and the captain and three members of the crew were rescued via rocket apparatus, the captain, Y.P. Klugkist, being most reluctant to leave. The schooner eventually moved further up the beach and became holed. This was the only rescue by the Volunteer Life Brigade during the war.

A new chief constable for Sunderland was appointed during 1915, namely F.S. Crawley, replacing Mr Carter, who had been in charge of the force since 1897. Mr Crawley brought some new ideas to the borough force, the main one being the introduction of police boxes, where prisoners could be housed temporarily, meals taken and clerical work done. In all, twenty-two boxes were erected around the town. Mr Crawley also introduced a probationary period for all new officers. In 1916, the first women joined the Borough Police Force.

Chief Constable F.S. Crawley, 1916.

Chapter Three

1916: Conscription, Zeppelin raids and shipwrecks

UP TO 1916, the Army relied on voluntary enlistment. However, there were decreasing numbers of men coming forward by the middle of 1915. In order to remedy the situation the Military Services Act came into force on 27 January, which introduced conscription to the country, except for Ireland. This applied to every male resident of the country who was nineteen but under the age of forty-one as of 15 August 1915. On 2 November, the category was narrowed to the effect that they had to be unmarried, or if widowed had to have no dependent children. There were exemptions to conscription, which were: if they were a resident of the dominions abroad or only living in the country for the purposes of their education; if they were members of the Royal Navy, Royal Marines or Army who were liable for foreign service but found to be unsuitable; men in holy orders or ministers of any religion; men of the armed forces who had been discharged on grounds of ill health or termination of engagement; and men who held a certificate of exemption or who had volunteered but had been turned down. Men could apply to a local tribunal for an exemption on the grounds of ill health, or if conscription would cause exceptional financial or business difficulties, or if it was in the national interest for him to continue his work or education, or on conscientious grounds. A man may be granted a temporary or absolute exemption. A Ryhope tenant farmer applied for an exemption on the grounds that, having foreign origins, he was unable to travel without police permission. His request was refused. A grocer applied for an absolute exemption on the grounds that he supported his widowed mother and deaf mute sister, his enlistment would cause financial hardship as the 4s 6d separation allowance would not be enough, and that his brother had enlisted. He was given a two-month extension. Conditional exemptions were given to a grazing and master shepherd, a wheelwright and a grocer's branch manager, being classified as reserved occupations, and also to a young van man, who was the sole supporter of his widowed mother and sister.

The introduction of conscription also brought into view conscientious objectors who refused to obey military orders for a number of reasons, be they religious or moral. Many conscientious objectors enlisted into the Non-Combatant Corps. The depot for the 2/Non-Combatant Corps was based at Richmond Castle, Yorkshire, and many objectors were sent there. An incident occurred in April that would eventually lead to a situation involving men who became known as the Richmond Sixteen. Initially, five conscientious objectors were arrested in Leeds and sent to Richmond, where they were locked up in the castle dungeon. More followed, until eventually sixteen men were being held there, including Norman Gaudie, from East Boldon, near Sunderland. (The other men were William and Herbert Law, John 'Bert' Brocklesby, Alfred Martlew, Clarence Hall, Horace Eaton, E.C. Cryer, C. Cartwright, C.R. Jackson, Alfred Myers, C.A. Senior, E.S. Spencer, Leonard Renton and J.W. Routledge; the name of the sixteenth man is not known.) Here they were treated badly, being fed on a diet of bread and water and subject to beatings. Eventually they were sent to France and told they were now on active service. One morning they were taken to the docks and ordered to unload a ship, which all but one refused to do, so they were charged with disobeying an order and subsequently court-martialled. All the men were found guilty and sentenced to death on 14 June. Lord Kitchener was keen to make an example of them but he was killed on 5 June while on his way to Russia; he was on board HMS *Hampshire* when it struck a mine and sank. The death sentences were commuted to ten years' hard labour by Prime Minister Herbert Asquith. Of the fifteen who went to prison, one died in prison, one escaped from Wormwood Scrubs and later drowned himself, and the others were released six months after the Armistice.

As with most other towns and cities, public transport in Sunderland was by tram. By 1916, no fewer than 111 men of those employed on the tram system before the war were serving in the forces and a further ten tram men were working in munitions. This shortfall in manpower on the tram system resulted in women being employed as conductors, the first ten being recruited on 9 June 1915. Eventually, all eighty-five wartime tram conductors were female and in 1918 women were employed as tram drivers, one being Annie Goodall. Training for five women drivers started on the Villette Road section on 3 March 1918. One of the problems that tram companies had to deal with was boys riding on the backs of trams. This had been almost eradicated before the outbreak of the war, but with the coming of female conductors the number of prosecutions for this offence rose to forty-five in a year. There were also four prosecutions for throwing things at tramcars and one for assaulting a female conductor. When the war was over and the men were demobilized the women gracefully retired from their jobs (or so it was claimed). By 1917, all the cleaning staff on the trams had been replaced by men exempt from military service. Tram services were also affected during the war. From 13 November 1916, all services stopped running after 10.30 pm (being cut back to 9.30 pm from 2 October 1918) and Sunday services ceased from 19 May 1918. This situation lasted until February 1919. As a fuel economy measure the number of stops was reduced.

Word came through that another member of the borough's police force had been killed in action. Private Thomas Meldrum, 18/Durham Light Infantry, was killed in action on 9 January by a bullet through the heart. Private Meldrum had been a constable at Sunderland Police Station, joining the force in October 1914. Prior to this he had served in the Border Regiment.

On 11 January, 160 (Wearside) Brigade RFA left for France, under the command of Colonel Warburton. For the previous three months the brigade had been at Cogton, Wiltshire, going there from Featherstone Park, Haltwhistle, and Salisbury Plain. The king had hoped to review the troops before their departure, but owing to his ill health he was not able to do so. Instead, a letter from him was read out by the officers.

The 20 (Wearside) Durham Light Infantry initially started its training at Wensley Camp, Wensleydale, but moved to Barnard Castle on 21 October 1915, where training became a lot more strenuous. The battalion reached full strength in December 1915, by which time it had become part of 123 Brigade, 41 Division. On 4 January 1916, it was taken over officially by the War Office and on the evening of that day, it left Barnard

Sunderland Central railway station, Union Street.

Castle for Aldershot, where it would complete its training. By April, the battalion was under orders to proceed overseas, so on 9 April the battalion left Aldershot for four days' farewell leave. For those who came back to Sunderland, they had a good send-off on 14 April. About 400 men paraded on the Town Moor, under Captain Wayman, and at 9.00 am, headed by the band of 4/Durham Light Infantry, marched to the town hall, Fawcett Street. Here they were addressed by the mayor, who was replied to by Lieutenant Colonel Leather. The parade then marched along Fawcett Street to the south end of Sunderland Central station, crowds lining the route. At the station they boarded a special train at 10.43 am for King's Cross. When they arrived in London, they marched across the city to Waterloo for the return train to Aldershot. Those who missed the parade that morning had to report to Captain Spencer at the south end of the Sunderland Central at 10.30 pm that evening. Only four men out of the whole battalion failed to turn up when ordered. Early in May, the battalion landed in France.

Zeppelin caught in searchlights.

For at least a century, the people of England had thought themselves to be safe, protected by the strength of the Royal Navy. Unfortunately, things were to change in this war. England had become vulnerable by attack from the air. Sunderland only suffered one air raid – a very serious one for the time, resulting in sixteen people being killed outright, twenty-five seriously injured, and four dying later. Eighty people were slightly injured.

The attack took place on Saturday night, 1 April 1916, April Fool's Day, and only one Zeppelin – the L11 – took part in it, crossing the coast at Seaham at a height of about 7,000 feet. It had left its base at Nordholz, along with L14, at midday with orders to attack southern or central England but the wind was such that the L11 found itself approaching the river Tyne in the dark. Following a Zeppelin raid on Tyneside by the L10 on 16 June 1915, the defences around the river Tyne had been strengthened. Because the L11 was at a relatively low height and was experiencing difficulties gaining height in the weather conditions, the commander, Korvettenkapitän Viktor Schütze, decided to manoeuvre round and attack the less well protected port of Sunderland. The L11 had dropped bombs at Hetton Downs, Eppleton and Philadelphia. These were evidently aimed at works in those vicinities, but no damage of any consequence was done and no casualties resulted. The machine then came on to Sunderland, which it reached a few minutes after 11.00 pm. The explosions at the villages had been heard by many in the town and subsequently people had been warned and were on the look-out.

It was a clear and starry night and when the Zeppelin was first seen over the west end of the town it was at an estimated height of 7,000 feet. It crossed the town in a north-easterly direction, its passage being of four to five minutes; during that time it dropped fourteen explosive and seven incendiary bombs. The first bomb fell in a yard in Back Peacock Street, at the west end of the town, but it did not explode. Others dropped in Pickard Street, Milburn Street and Fern Street. After this the Zeppelin crossed the river Wear, where the river bends to the south, and, arriving over Monkwearmouth, threw bombs into the Monkwearmouth goods yard as well as into North Bridge Street, The Causeway, Victor Street and the shipyard of Messrs John Bulmer & Co. The greatest amount of damage was done in Fern Street, North Bridge Street and Victor Street.

When first built there was a roof over the railway lines between the main building at Monkwearmouth Station and the goods yard on the west side. This roof provided shelter for the passengers waiting for their trains. A casualty of the raid was this roof over the railway lines and it was never repaired, being removed completely twelve years later in 1928, when the platform shelters for the passengers were built. The bombs narrowly missed the new fire engine for the borough, which was still standing on a wagon in the station goods yard.

The bomb that fell in North Bridge Street was responsible for more victims than any other single bomb that was dropped on the town. As a result, five people were either killed outright or died from their injuries within a day or two.

One of the victims was Mr Thomas Shepherd Dale (aged fifty-five), a borough magistrate, a building manager living in Monkwearmouth, and a leader of the local Labour Party who was a group leader engaged in special constable duty at the time. In another case a man was walking along a street with two of his daughters, one on each arm, while just in front of him his wife was walking with two other women. When the bomb exploded, one of the daughters was hurled through a plate-glass window and killed. The other women of the party were injured, but the man was not touched.

As there had been warning of the impending attack the trams had been evacuated, as was the practice. Although the company's regulations stated that the conductor should remain with the tram, to this end, Miss Margaret Ann Holmes (aka Sally Ann Holmes) gallantly carried out her duties to the full and as a result she suffered a serious injury to her right leg. After months in hospital she returned to a job in the tramway office.

The North Bridge Street bomb blast caused extensive damage to property. Tramcar No. 10 had been pulled up in the street and was wrecked, along with a house. A tramway employee here had a narrow escape as he and an inspector took refuge against a wall, the inspector being the one nearest the wall. A piece of shrapnel flew over the outer man's shoulder and went through the heart of the inspector.

The other two districts in which there were large numbers of casualties were Millfield and Victor Street, Monkwearmouth, where two seventeen-year-olds perished, namely Florence May Johnson and John Glasgow. At a shop in Victor Street a bomb explosion killed three people, two of them being brothers: Thomas (aged fifty-five) and George (aged fifty-three) Holmes Rogerson, both single and both grocers. Their shop was open late, until nearly midnight. They and a girl who was a customer at the time of the attack were found lying dead in the debris. In this vicinity too, a man was carrying his family downstairs away from the attack and, as he was bringing the last one down and was being followed by his son, the upper part of the house was struck and wrecked. The boy was killed; the father and other children escaped.

Many miraculous escapes were recorded, the majority being due to the presence of mind of people who threw themselves flat on the ground when they saw the flash that accompanied the dropping of the bombs, and by doing so they escaped the flying fragments of glass and metal. In several cases a house was practically blown to pieces by a bomb and yet all those inside escaped unhurt. It was shown at victims' inquests that in the majority of cases, death was due to wounds on the body caused by pieces of flying glass. For this reason it was pointed out that it was safer for people to remain indoors in an attack than to go outside, although in the North Bridge Street raid there were more people killed indoors than outdoors, owing to the fact that the bombs had been dropped on a densely populated locality.

The chief buildings damaged were the Workmen's Hall, Monkwearmouth, which was practically demolished, Thomas Street Council School, which was partially demolished, and St Benet's Roman Catholic Church, which had its doors damaged and most of its windows blown out, including a valuable, coloured-glass memorial window. Also damaged were the Thompson Memorial Hall, Dundas Street, which had windows broken, and the Corporation Tramways Sheds, Wheatsheaf. Eight business premises were demolished and two partially demolished, fifteen dwelling houses were demolished and sixty-six partly so, and 158 houses and sixty-four shops had windows blown in and other minor damage. The damage was chiefly confined to homes inhabited by working-class people who in many instances had all or part of their furniture destroyed or damaged.

There were four outbreaks of fires in connection with the raid; three of them were quite trivial and were extinguished by people in the vicinity, while the fourth was at Messrs John Bulmer & Co's shipyard, where a French polishing shop was set on fire and burned down. A ship in the course of construction at this yard was also damaged – the only instance in which any industrial work suffered or damage was done that might be considered of value from an enemy point of view. The Fire Brigade was called to the Wearmouth Colliery, where the bombs had set fire to some railway sleepers on the staithes, causing slight damage. The Fire Brigade were also called to Fern Street, but this turned out to be a false alarm.

Two shots were fired at the Zeppelin from guns in the neighbourhood, but it was not hit, and it was stated that some hitch occurred that prevented anything further being done. Having come under fire from a gun at Fulwell, the Zeppelin turned to the south-east and after dropping bombs on the docks flew down to Middlesbrough, where it caused more destruction, injuring two people, before returning to base at Nordholz at 10.00 am on 2 April.

The following is a list of those who lost their lives in the attack. The trail of the Zeppelin can virtually be traced by the victims' addresses:

Name	Address	Age	Occupation	Buried (where known)
Thomas Shepherd Dale	83, Forster Street, Monkwearmouth	55	Building manager	Mere Knolls
Thomas Rogerson	12, Brandling Street	55	Grocer	
George Holmes Rogerson	12, Brandling Street	53	Grocer	
John Glasgow	65, Victor Street	17		Mere Knolls
Florence May Johnson	57, Victor Street	17		Mere Knolls
Joseph Thompson	29, Roxburgh Street	46	Tramway motorman	Mere Knolls
Henry Patrick	12, Eden Street North	16		Mere Knolls
Gertrude Ann Patrick	12, Eden Street North	19		Mere Knolls
Alfred Finkle	32, Dame Dorothy Street	39	House plumber	Mere Knolls
Herbert Archibald Chater	141, Victor Street	47		
Elizabeth Weldon	2, The Causeway	67		Mere Knolls
Elizabeth Ann Ranson	3, The Causeway	5		Mere Knolls
Alfred Wood Dunlop	6, Howick Street	17	Scholar	Mere Knolls
Ernest Liddle Johnstone	12, Fern Street	31	Patternmaker engineer	Bishopwearmouth died 2 APRIL
John Joseph Woodward	11, Fern Street	38	Boiler maker	
Elizabeth Jane Thirkell	12, Burlington Road	16	Scholar	Grangetown, Sunderland
John Thomas Lydon	21, Fern Street	14	Scholar	
Hanna Lydon	21, Fern Street	33		
Henry Dean	16, Derwent Street	28		
Robert Garbutt Fletcher	2, North Bridge Street	68	Furniture dealer	Mere Knolls

In addition, a number of deaths occurred that were recorded as due, more or less, to shock arising from the raid.

Although any fires caused were quickly extinguished and material damage was not great, the greater effect had been on the morale of the population, which had been shaken. However, Korvettenkapitän Viktor Schütze of the Zeppelin L11 thought differently and reported as such:

I decided not to cross the batteries on account of not being very high in relation to the firing, and also because of slow progress against the wind and the absolutely clear atmosphere up above. I fixed, therefore, on the town of Sunderland, with its extensive docks and the blast furnaces north-west of the town. Keeping on the weather side, the airships [*sic*] dropped explosive bombs on some works where one blast furnace was blown up with a terrible detonation, sending out flames and smoke. The factories and dock buildings of Sunderland, now brightly illuminated, were then bombed with good results. The effect was grand; blocks of houses and rows of streets collapsed entirely; large fires broke out in places and a dense black

General view near the Wheatsheaf tram depot.

cloud, from which bright sparks flew high, was caused by one bomb. A second explosive bomb was at once dropped at the same spot; judging from the situation, it may have been a railway station.

The official reaction to the raid was a communiqué stating that 'bombs were dropped at various places but no details are at present available.' Sir Hiram Maxim, famed for the Maxim machine gun, said of the attack: 'I still lean to the view that we in Great Britain should work on lines of producing things which will destroy Zeppelins rather than produce Zeppelins ourselves. But of course it is essential in the interests of a proper decision on this and every other point connected with flying that there should be an air ministry with a scientific statesman at its head.'

The chief constable later gave the following advice in case of future air raids: 'Indications that enemy aircraft are in the vicinity are as follows: first, the cutting off of the electrical supply, second, the noise caused by the explosion of bombs.'

The day after this incident advertisements appeared in the local press offering insurance against damage caused by Zeppelin raids. Not only could you get cover for business premises, starting from 6s 9d, and private premises from 5s and 9d, but also insurance to cover death, loss of two limbs, blindness and various other combinations

Sally Holmes, a tram conductress who was injured in the Zeppelin raid.

Tram conductress Liza Smith.

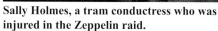

of injury. Prices on application!

The funerals of the first victims took place on 5 April, with window blinds being closed in residences, large crowds lining the route to pay tribute and flags being flown

Tram No. 10 destroyed in the air raid of April 1916.

The Roker acoustic mirror, one of a chain along the North East coast, built following the air raids.

City of Sunderland

COASTAL WATCH MIRROR

This convex dish detected German Zeppelins sent to bomb north – east ports. Their course could be judged from engine sounds focussed onto a receiver, giving 15 minutes warning for anti – aircraft defences to be directed onto them.

World War I Defences

Blue plaque on the side of the acoustic mirror.

at half-mast.

The L11 had made its first flight on 7 June 1915 and went on to complete thirty-one reconnaissance missions, notably during the naval Battle of Jutland (31 May 1916) and twelve raids on England. It was was decommissioned in April 1917.

On several later occasions, Zeppelins were reported within a comparatively short distance of Sunderland and every preparation was made in the expectation of an attack, which fortunately never occurred.

This was not the only raid by Zeppelins on the North East coast, but the only one where Sunderland was bombed. On 8/9 August 1916, the L14 crossed the coast at Tweedmouth at 12.25 am, made a wide sweep as far west as Kelso and then headed out to sea at Alnmouth at 2.00 am. The bombs fell on open country; only eight craters were found. At 12.55 am, the L30 made landfall at Hartlepool, dropped bombs around Seaton Carew and then flew back out to sea. The L13 crossed the coast at 1.30 am, dropped bombs around Wingate and Thornley, and flew out to sea at 2.05 am near Hawthorn. At 1.45 am, the L31 crossed the coast south of Whitburn, flew in a loop over South Shields, North Shields and Jarrow before heading back out to sea near Marsden at 2.00 am.

Finally, the L11 appeared briefly over Tynemouth and Whitley Bay. The only effects of these raids were five people injured at Whitley Bay and a house and office wrecked. In addition to this, the L35 – designated a 'Super Zeppelin' – crossed the coast south of Seaham on her maiden flight on the night of 27/28 November, and then turned and headed back home.

Although Zeppelins had the range to raid England they were at the mercy of the weather and winds and were also vulnerable to attack by aircraft and anti-aircraft guns. From a total of 115 Zeppelins used against England, seventy-seven were either destroyed or so badly damaged that they were not used again. No Zeppelin raids took place after June 1917.

As a result of these, and several other air raids by Zeppelins and aeroplanes on the country, the military began to install defences along the coast. One such precaution was acoustic mirrors, which, it is believed, were placed in positions from the Humber to the Tyne. One of these mirrors was built at Fulwell, just over a mile from the sea. Each mirror comprised a 15-foot concave shape cut into a concrete wall, which was inclined, with two other smaller stabilizing walls that also served to protect it against other noises. The wall was about 19 feet long and 13 feet high. The mirror reflected the sound of approaching Zeppelins into a microphone positioned in front of it, and the position was then plotted by an observer who was in a trench nearby. This system was designed to give fifteen minutes' warning of the approach of the enemy. This mirror was of the Coastal Watcher type and was used up until the mid-1930s. In addition to this, anti-aircraft batteries were sited around the town.

Admiral Scheer, the commander of the German Imperial Navy, drew up plans to draw the British Grand Fleet out from its bases in Scotland into an ambush by his submarines on 17 May. The central theme for this trap was for a number of German battlecruisers, to include the *Seydlitz*, which should have come out of dry dock, to shell Sunderland. Unfortunately for Scheer, the *Seydlitz* was not ready on time and the operation was postponed until 30 May. German U-boats had been on station the entire time and by the end of May were running short of fuel. The decision was taken to recall the submarines, which meant that the ambush did not take place. Instead, the German High Seas Fleet

SMS *Seydlitz*, which was to have taken part in the raid on Sunderland in 1916.

(Hochseeflotte) left harbour, as did the Grand Fleet, and the action at Jutland was the result.

In France, the Battle of the Somme opened on 1 July after seven days' preparatory bombardment, resulting in the British Army suffering its greatest number of casualties in one day in its history, the total being 60,000, of which more than 19,000 were killed. Many of the Pals battalions suffered heavily with, in some instances, the equivalent of every other house in a street receiving a telegram to say a brother, husband or son had been killed or wounded. The battle was to drag on until November, with the British Army suffering more than 400,000 casualties.

Prior to the war, the idea of women working in factories was not a popular one and they would definitely have not been paid the same rate as men were. When the Ministry of Munitions was established under David Lloyd George in 1915, the practices that prevented women from working in industry were removed. By 1916, more women industrial workers were needed, especially after the casualties suffered on the Somme and the introduction of conscription. Many women worked in munitions; they were known as munitionettes and received half the pay of their male colleagues. Some women found it was a way to escape from domestic drudgery as well as a way of gaining employment and companionship. By early 1917, almost eighty per cent of munitions workers were female.

One of the many sports and social events that were organized for women workers at this time was football; there were no formal leagues, but friendly matches between factories, many drawing big crowds. Proceeds from the events went to charitable concerns, including the Sunderland hospitals. Tyneside had nine different ladies teams;

Sunderland had three main teams: Glaholm, Robson & Co; Webster & Co; and Sunderland Ladies. The latter was formed following an advertisement in the *Sunderland Daily Echo* in September 1917. On Boxing Day 1917, a match took place between Webster's Ropery and Glaholm & Robson Ropery to raise funds for the Durham Light Infantry Prisoners of War Fund.

As the war ended and the men returned to their jobs, thus replacing women in industry, so the munitionettes teams faded away. The last known games of the Sunderland Ladies were against Newcastle Ladies in May 1919, when Newcastle Ladies won both. At the game that took place at Roker Park, a total of £346 was raised for charity, although it is not known how much was raised at the game at St James's Park.

The men's professional leagues had been suspended after the 1914-15 season, partly due to lack of interest and partly to the players enlisting. Charlie Buchan, who played for Sunderland, joined the Sherwood Foresters initially and then

Charles Buchan, a Sunderland player from 1911 to 1925. He won the Military Medal while serving with the Grenadier Guards.

transferred to the Grenadier Guards. It was with them that he won the Military Medal.

The long-awaited naval engagement between the Royal Navy and the German High Seas Fleet took place on 31 May and 1 June, at the Battle of Jutland. It was said of Admiral Lord Jellicoe that he was the only man in the country who could win or lose the war in a single afternoon. The opening phase of the action involved the battlecruisers of the Grand Fleet with the German battleships. During the engagement, HMS *Invincible*, HMS *Queen Mary* and HMS *Indefatigable* each blew up after being hit by German broadsides, which caused Admiral Beattie, the force commander, to say: 'There is something wrong with our bloody ships today.'

Out of a total complement of 1,031 men on board HMS *Invincible*, only six survived. There were at least four men from Sunderland killed aboard the ship: Shipwright 2nd Class Joseph Watson, from Fulwell Road, Monkwearmouth; Stoker First Class A. Ross; Leading Stoker W.E. Riddell; and Ordinary Seaman W. Parkinson. HMS *Queen Mary* had a crew of 1,266, of which only twenty survived. Of those killed, at least seven came from Sunderland: Petty Officer J. Connelly; Stokers 1st Class J. Darling, M.J. Lambert and C.M. Russell; Stoker 2nd Class G. Paxton; and Able Seamen J.C. Emmerson and W.R. Jefferis. In addition, Sunderland men serving on other ships were killed during the battle. Both sides claimed the battle as a victory. Although the British lost more ships and men than the Germans, the German fleet didn't venture out to sea until after the war, when it was taken to Scapa Flow in the Orkneys. It was here that it it surrendered to the Allies and later 'committed suicide' by the crews scuttling their ships.

On 11 July, a U-boat appeared off the coast of Seaham, moving to within 400 yards of the town. It proceeded to fire between twenty and forty shells into the town and surrounding fields. Only one person, Mary Slaughter, aged thirty-five of Hebburn, was killed as she was walking through the Colliery Yard with a friend. At the time she was badly injured and died in hospital the next day. At one property a nose of a shell passed through the back wall and hit the front door. Luckily, nobody was injured. The boat then left the area, on the surface.

In October, the authorities established an airfield between Sunderland and Washington, on the north side of the river Wear. The airfield was originally called Hylton, or West Town Aerodrome, but was later renamed RAF Usworth. It was here that B Flight of 36 (Home Defence) Squadron was based. Initially the squadron was equipped with BE2cs and BE12s, and their task was to protect the coast between Whitby and Newcastle-upon-Tyne. During 1918, A Flight moved to RAF Usworth, with headquarters following in November, from Cramlington, by which time it had been equipped with a more modern aircraft, the Bristol F2bs. RAF Usworth is now the site of the Nissan car works.

A memorial service took place at the Moor Street Synagogue on 31 October, at which civic and military dignitaries were present to commemorate four Jewish soldiers who had been killed at the front. In his sermon the rabbi mentioned that 150 Jewish men from Sunderland had already enlisted; a total of sixteen died.

A story of bravery in a very young seaman was reported in the local press. Harry Craggs Forrest, born on 30 September 1900, an apprentice from Sunderland, was serving aboard a local steamer when it was attacked by a submarine. The incident took place on

SS *Capelcastle* in her wartime dazzle paint. Dazzle paint was designed to make it difficult for submarine commanders to determine a ship's outline, course and speed, which were measurements needed in calculating the course of a torpedo.

21 November 1916, and was mentioned by Lord Jellicoe as an example of the gallantry of the Mercantile Marine. Just before 2.00 pm the submarine was sighted about 100 yards behind the ship. Forrest was engaged in steering the ship, having taken over from a fellow crewman who had been taken ill. The captain immediately gave the order for the ship to steer a zigzag course. The Germans opened fire and hit the ship. It was thought that the shell had hit below the waterline. The crew took shelter from the shrapnel wherever they could, but the captain and Forrest remained exposed on the bridge. A fire broke out, which the crew managed to extinguish, and another shell injured a crewman. During the engagement Forrest was wounded, shrapnel causing a nasty scalp wound and splitting his cap from side to side. He was unaware that he had been hit. Throughout the incident the captain and young Forrest stayed on the bridge steering the ship, which eventually pulled away from the submarine and made it safely to port. The whole action lasted about an hour. For his bravery Harry Craggs Forrest was awarded the Distinguished Service Medal. He sent his cap home to his mother as a souvenir, together with a piece of shrapnel that still had some of his hair on it.

Chapter Four

1917: U-boats, hospitals, air crashes – and a royal visit

EARLY IN THE year, on 23 February, one of those unfortunate freak incidents took place when the German submarine UC32 was blown up by one of the mines it had just laid off the mouth of the river Wear. At 6.30 pm the submarine had laid its first mine and was cruising on the surface when an explosion occurred under its hull. It is thought that the plug holding the mine to the sinker had dissolved prematurely, releasing the mine under her stern end. Only three of the crew escaped – Oberlieutenant Herbert Breyer, Oberstauermansmaat Skau and Oberheizer Reinhard Schirm, all of whom became prisoners of war. Reinhard Schirm left an account of his rescue in a letter to his mother. In it he says:

> I was in the control room. The explosion extinguished the lights immediately and I was hurled forward owing to the pressure of the water flooding in (for the boat had been torn in half). I was driven upwards. I held my breath. At the same moment the bottles containing compressed air burst and I was thrown into the conning tower. As for the moment the pressure was greater from inside than outside, I could take breath again. The boat in the meantime had sunk to the bottom. I let go and was thrown out.
>
> I swam on the surface 200 metres from the boat. I shouted for help and found my strength failing me (I had not slept for some 28 hours) and had swallowed a good deal of oil. I also had my heavy leather clothing and sea boots on. I took my boots off and managed to pull one leg out of my leather breeches but swallowed

German mine-laying submarine UC5, similar to the UC32, which was blown up by one of its own mines in February 1917.

a great quantity of oil in the process; now for the other leg. Because my hands were quite numb I could not get my knife out, but somehow I managed to get my remaining leg out of the leather breeches with some difficulty. I felt my limbs stiffening with the cold. I shouted for help again.

At last I saw a light and soon after a second one. The first was the Sunderland [*sic*] lighthouse, the second the light of an English patrol boat. I swam towards it and when I was about 20 yards off someone threw me a lifebelt. An English sailor handed me an oar and pulled me into his boat. I heard a voice: 'Hullo Schirm, you here too?' I recognized the captain. There were only three of us.

We were very well looked after on a steamer and the English sailors were kind to us. They must have felt sorry for us because they kept giving us their cigarettes. My English helped a bit. We were given dry clothes and in the evening taken to hospital. Again we were kindly treated and well fed, but we were strictly guarded. On Sunday we were taken to the station.

Shortly after the sinking the Navy started to dive on the wreck hoping to find code books, loose articles and anything that might have been of interest. They found that the forward section of the boat was intact, although the hull near the engine room was severely damaged. Visibility was bad. Lieutenant Commander Guybon C.C. Damant was in charge of the salvage operation. By the middle of March they had retrieved a torpedo, complete with warhead. However, by the end of the month diving had been halted because it was thought that there was nothing else to learn and it was appreciated that there were still fourteen unexploded mines on board. The UC32 had sunk six ships during its career, some of them off the mouth of the Wear.

During the winter of 1916/17, the War Office asked the town of Sunderland if it would undertake the building of a military hospital comprising 500-600 beds. This was a large undertaking and the sensibilities of the VAD hospitals had to be taken into consideration. Two of the town's leading surgeons visited Leeds and other areas to view construction of this type of hospital and their final report proved invaluable to the committee responsible. A public meeting was held in January 1917, at which the appeal fund was launched, and by the end of February, £28,000 of the required £30,000 had been raised. The government had also promised £10,000 towards equipping it. The hospital stood on land belonging to the Sunderland Board of Guardians and included some of the old Union Workhouse. Due to the urgency of building the hospital, five contractors were used; surprisingly there were no major problems. By May, six pavilions were completed and the first wounded arrived on 27 August. The official opening did not take place until 25 September 1917 and was performed by Lieutenant General John Maxwell, Northern Command. Also present were Lady Maxwell and Major General Kerr Montgomery of the Tyne Garrison as well as several other officers and council members.

May 1917 saw tragedy visit Southwick. During a food economy meeting held in the evening of 24 May on The Green an aeroplane crashed into the Sunderland Co-operative Society premises. The aeroplane then fell into the crowd that had gathered to hear the address. Five people were killed; two outright, one being a little boy having a portion of his head cut off. Eight others were injured. Most of the injured were taken to the Royal Infirmary, but Mrs Brannigan was taken to Monkwearmouth Hospital for treatment.

The Co-op building at The Green, Southwick.

The aeroplane, from 36 Squadron, based at Usworth Airfield, just outside the town, was flown by Lieutenant Philip Thompson.

He had set out earlier for the coast to test the newly fitted machine guns on his aircraft. On his way back to the airfield he noticed the crowd on The Green. It appears that he decided to do a few stunts to entertain them, but due to the position of the sun he unfortunately did not see a large flag pole in the centre of The Green. The impact broke the propeller and stopped the engine. In addition, his left wing was torn off by the pole, causing him to crash into the Co-operative building, breaking the drapery department window at the corner of Stoney Lane. The plane had already flown over the meeting twice before the accident happened. A weather vane in the shape of a ship that had been mounted on the top of the flag pole was found 57 yards away. The flag pole itself was not damaged, but the flag had fallen to half-mast.

Lieutenant Philip Thompson, pilot of the aircraft that crashed at Southwick in May 1917.

The following is a list of those killed and injured:

Killed

Elizabeth Curry (forty-nine), of 28, Grosvenor Street, Southwick, wife of George Curry, a patternmaker at iron foundry, injured on head.

Robert Spargo (eleven), son of Robert Spargo, labourer in shipyard, living at 27, Nelson Street, Southwick, severe injuries to the head, part of which was taken off.

John Connelly (twenty-nine), of 25, Alice Street, Southwick, recently married, injuries to head, died at 10.50 pm, ship plater at Messrs Priestmans.

John Thompson (eighty), widower, wood carver and gilder, of 16, Camden Street, Southwick, injuries to head, died at 1.50 am.

George Davison (forty-seven), of 16, Cowper Street, Southwick, injuries to face, head and fractured ribs, died at 11.50 pm, insurance agent.

Injured

Ellen Rowell (fourteen), of 7, Ogle Street, Southwick, shock and concussion.

Thomas Corner (twenty-one), of 13, Malaburn Street, Southwick, shoulder injured, miner at Hylton Colliery.

Robert Peary (fifty-four), of 8, Cowper Street, Southwick, injuries to head and face, labourer at Messrs Priestmans.

Isabella Unwin (fifty-eight), of 26, Abbey Street, Southwick, injuries to arm, wife of joiner at Messrs Priestmans.

Annie Cullerton (seventeen), of King's Road, Southwick, injuries to arms and face, employed at Messrs Swan and Hunters, Southwick.

William Hodgson (thirteen), of 4, Church Street, Monkwearmouth, son of a soldier, concussion.

Bernard Smith (ten), of 3, Wellington Street, Southwick, son of a riveter at Messrs Doxford's, lacerated leg.

Elizabeth Brannigan (seventy-six), of 12, Malaburn Terrace, Southwick, injuries to head and shock.

The funeral of Robert Spargo took place on 27 May, when he was interred in Southwick Cemetery. The funeral was well attended. Alongside his relatives were Inspector Banks, Sergeant Heald and PC Danby of the Southwick Police, and Messrs J.W. Trueman and W.J. Habberley representing the Southwick War Savings and Food Control Committee. Among the wreaths was a floral tribute from the Royal Flying Corps.

At the inquest it was revealed that the flying station had been asked if one of the planes could fly over the food economy meeting, but this request had not been passed on to the pilots. Sergeant Flynn of the Durham County Constabulary said in giving evidence that the airman had perfect control of the aeroplane until it hit the flagpole. Lieutenant Thompson, who had joined the Royal Flying Corps on 22 April 1916 and had qualified as a pilot on 14 July 1916, told the inquest that on his way to the coast to test his guns he had noticed a crowd on The Green. Having successfully carried out his tests, on his return he found that the crowd was still there. He planed down towards the fields, passing over The Green. The sun was in his eyes as he was flying west and it was fairly windy. Being partially blinded by the sun, he misjudged the distances as he tried to clear the flagstaff. Captain Joseph Clifford Griffiths, Flying Station Commander, said that he had made no promise to fly over the meeting and did not mention it to the aviator. He also mentioned that Lieutenant Thompson was a careful and a very good pilot, having had considerable experience, including four months in France. Captain Griffiths had been out with the same machine on the afternoon of that day as far as Easington and had found it in perfect order, as was the engine. The machine was later taken to the aerodrome. On examination Captain Griffiths found that the engine was split right down the centre, having evidently struck something very hard – concrete or stone. Other portions were also damaged. There had been absolutely nothing faulty about the biplane prior to the accident.

In his summing up Mr Shepherd, the coroner, said:

In the middle of a great war and that in which the Royal Flying Corps were playing a very important and highly successful part, not only in fighting the enemy but in helping protect our coast against hostile aircraft. [The RFC's] help was much appreciated in recent attacks on the North East coast and they must carry on their work under all conditions and situations in order to become perfectly efficient in their work. At the same time they must have regard to the safety of the public and must not expose them to unnecessary risk.

Most of the jury had been present at the meeting at the time of the accident. The jury took only a few minutes to reach a verdict, the foreman announcing: 'We find accidental death in both cases and exonerate the airman from all blame.' Lieutenant Thompson was exceedingly sorry that he should have been in any way associated, although following his military duties, with causing the deaths. Although exonerated from blame, the sad occurrence would be a lifelong regret for Lieutenant Thompson. Unfortunately, this was not to be for very long: he returned to France in March 1918 and was killed in action on the 23rd of that month while on an offensive patrol over Cambrai, serving with 22 Squadron RFC. His Bristol aircraft was shot down, his observer being taken prisoner.

In June, the king and queen came to the North East of England, visiting shipyards and engineering works to thank the workers for their contribution towards the war effort. On 15 June, the royal couple came to Sunderland. The previous day they had visited Teesside and Hartlepool and at 6.00 pm that night the Royal Train passed through Sunderland Central station, which was closed for the event. It was a glorious day and crowds lined the streets to obtain a glimpse of the royal couple. The day was not declared a holiday as the king wished to see the shipyards and engineering works in full production.

The royal party arrived in the town just before 10.00 am, from Southwick, and were driven down High Street East to the docks. At the North Eastern Marine Engineering Co Ltd, South Dock, the royal party were introduced to the Earl of Durham, Lord Lieutenant of the county; the mayor and mayoress of the town, Mr and Mrs W.F. Vint, and their daughter, Mrs A.G. Taylor; Mr. H. Craven, town clerk; Mr Ralph Milbanke Hudson, chairman of the River Wear Commission; Mr James Marr, chairman of the Wear Shipbuilders' Association; and a member of the Advisory Committee to the Deputy Controller of Auxiliary Shipping, Admiralty. The king shook hands with each person and exchanged a few pleasantries. He said, 'I know how important the Borough of Sunderland is, and I was most anxious to see its industries, and I am only too glad to have the opportunity to do so.'

The machines in the works were in full operation as the royal couple passed, stopping occasionally to watch a particular item being made and entering into conversation with individual employees. Mr Summers Hunter (Managing Director) and Mr Weir (Manager of the Works) explained things as they progressed. The king noticed a wounded soldier who was employed on light duties and asked him where in France he had been wounded, receiving the reply: 'At the Battle of Hooge' (9 August 1915). The king then wished him a speedy recovery.

In some of the workshops the heat was intense and the king and queen had to shelter their faces with their hands, especially near the rolling of a boiler end plate. One of the workmen moved away from the roller, breathing heavily and sweating freely. He was seen to have his legs wrapped to protect them from the heat. When asked what the wrappings were called, he replied 'bags'. During his tour the king spoke to Mr William Robert Humphrys, who informed the king that he had lost his son, Arthur Easton Humphrys, killed in action on 8 May 1917 while serving with 18/Durham Light Infantry. (Private Humphrys had originally enlisted in 20/Durham Light Infantry.) The king expressed his sorrow for his loss.

The making of a huge nut, being turned by William Charlton, especially caught the attention of the royal party, who watched the operation carefully, in spite of the heat. On their tour through the factory the king and queen were cheered by the workforce, as well as by men on the quay and on a ship on the river. At the end of the tour, just as he was about to board the car, the king spoke to Mr Summers Hunter saying that the works he had seen were very fine and that he had great pleasure in his visit and the attitude of those employed there.

Their next visit was to Sir James Laing and Sons Ltd, Deptford Yard, shipbuilders and brass founders, arriving there at approximately 11.00 am. Laing's was one of the oldest shipbuilders on the river, specialists in oil tank steamers (several of which were under construction at the time) as well as in standard steamers of 8,000 tons, and other cargo vessels. The firm employed 1,100 men and forty women.

Again, the royal party was greeted by Mr James Marr, who presented His Majesty to officials of the yard. As before, the king and queen were greeted by cheers as they toured the yards. Everyone was working, only those who spoke to the royal couple stopping for a short time. The king took a keen interest in the merchant ships being built, which were at various stages of construction. The first part of the visit was to the joinery shop, where men, young women and girls worked. Here the king had a good laugh at the expense of one of the girls. Mr Laing, who was conducting the king and queen round, was explaining a tenoning machine. The king noticed that some of the wood shavings being expelled from the machine were sticking to the hair of the girl working on the next machine. He also appreciated a chalked message on the side of a ship being built that read, 'We will deliver the ships'.

While watching the riveters at work the king noticed a young lad of small stature, not much bigger than a walking stick. He asked him how old he was and the lad replied seventeen, which surprised the king. The lad's name was John Cassidy; he worked in the foreman's office and started as a messenger boy. The king was introduced to Walter Moffat Fairgrieve, who had been a furnaceman for sixty years, he being eighty-two. He had only missed two periods of work, one due to an accident and the other when the yard was closed. It had been estimated that Fairgrieve had shovelled about 70,000 tons of coal during his working life.

The king and queen expressed their pleasure in the visit to Mr Hugh Laing before leaving to visit Messrs W. Doxford & Sons Ltd, Pallion Shipyards. Doxford's was one of the largest firms of shipbuilders and engineers in the country. They were working for the Admiralty and building merchant ships, as well as being busy with experimental work in new engines. They employed about 4,000 people in the Pallion yard.

The royal visit, 1917.

After being shown round the offices, the king and queen saw all aspects of work done at the yard and were especially interested in the electric cranes that lifted heavy material and a great electrical saw, which was operated by two young girls. The royal couple were shown ships under construction and examined a vessel tied up to the dock.

Their Majesties visit William Doxford's in June 1917.

Although the royal procession's itinerary had only been issued to the press, it had somehow leaked out to the public, who were lining the route and had covered all the best vantage points from early in the day. Some parts of the route were densely packed, such as 'Mackie's Corner'. The police were out in force, many wearing military decorations, and were aided by a number of special constables. Bunting was in evidence everywhere, especially in the East End. When passing Sunderland Technical College, a party of fifty-six wounded soldiers and their nurses were seated along the pavement. As the royal car approached it slowed down and the king saluted the men and women, which pleased everyone.

Refreshments were taken at Doxford's, after which the king and queen returned to the Royal Train at Southwick by motor for lunch, stopping on Alexandra Bridge to obtain a general view of the shipyards. During the afternoon the royal couple visited Messrs Joseph

The king and queen visiting a shipyard in June 1917.

L. Thompson & Sons Ltd, North Sands, shipbuilders. This firm was mainly concerned with mercantile shipbuilding and employed 1,200 people. Then there was a visit to Messrs John Crown & Co, shipbuilders, who almost exclusively built colliers. At 3.30 pm the king and queen went to Messrs George Clark Ltd, marine engine builders, who were doing a lot of work for the Admiralty, with 1,200 men and eighty women being employed at the yard. The final visit of the day was to Messrs William Pickersgill & Sons, shipbuilders, who built mainly merchant ships. After a long day the king and queen left for their train at 4.40 pm.

The mayor received the following letter dated 15 June 1917 from the Royal Train:

Dear Mr Mayor,

The king and queen were greatly impressed with the busy life of Sunderland and much regret that time did not admit of further visits to shipbuilding and engineering firms.

Their Majesties were very glad to have this chance of seeing for themselves the contribution that the men and women of the district are making towards our common effort.

The police arrangements were well planned and carried out, and the king did not fail to observe the number of special constables on duty.

Their Majesties were much gratified with their reception and have carried away the happiest memory of the loyalty and devotion of the people of Sunderland, and of their visit to the great industries on the banks of the Wear.

Yours very truly

Clive Wigram

Cheering crowds greet the queen as she visits Wearside.

The king meets John Cassidy.

Chapter Five

1918: The storm before the calm
Of ships and funds and a tank called *Nelson*

SATURDAY, 12 JANUARY saw a disaster involving a ship that had been built at Doxford's shipyards in 1915/16. HMS *Opal*, part of 12 Destroyer Flotilla, in company with the light cruiser HMS *Boadicea* and *Opal*'s sister ship HMS *Narborough*, were carrying out a dark night patrol off Scotland, hunting for auxiliary German cruisers that were suspected of laying mines. Unfortunately the weather was atrocious and visibility was down to zero. Both of the destroyers were in danger of being swamped and foundering, with the real possibility of sinking. They were ordered to return to port, while HMS *Boadicea* continued alone. Regular radio contact was received from *Opal* until 9.27 pm, when a garbled message was received stating that she had run aground. *Opal* was found two days later on the rocks of the Clett of Crura, Orkney, battered and broken, with masts and funnel gone. HMS *Narborough* was found nearby in a similar state. Of the two ships' crews, only one man survived. It was thought that the tragedy had happened as a result of a navigational error by the captain. The wrecks were sold for scrap in the 1930s.

Throughout the war food economy campaigns were run to encourage people not to waste food and ensure every scrap was used. This became more pressing from 1917 onwards when the Germans unleashed their U-boats and declared unrestricted use of these undersea weapons, which resulted in heavy losses of merchant shipping. Food economy demonstrations were given throughout Sunderland, especially in the workplace

A destroyer ploughing through a gale.

and in the theatres during the evenings. These demonstrations proved very popular and at times some of the women wanting to attend were turned away because there was no room for them. Even the children were involved, with the setting up of the Children's Food Saving League. Each member received a badge, and it was not long before the badges were seen all over the town. When the war broke out it was suggested that vacant land could be turned to cultivation and people could be given allotments. This was a popular move and resulted in allotment associations springing up around the town.

The government introduced rationing in February, as a direct result of the U-boat war. By May, butter, cheese and margarine were added to the list of rationed items. Everyone had to be registered with a butcher and grocer, and ration cards were issued. The introduction of this system was seen by some to be beneficial, as everyone now had a fair chance. As can be imagined, there was profiteering. Percy Newman was given a 16-stone bag of sugar to make sarsaparilla; instead he repackaged it and sold it to customers in his other shops. He was charged with selling sugar without the appropriate certificate and fined £35 – £5 for each offence. He was not the only person to be punished for this offence; his female assistants were bound over for helping.

Throughout the war different initiatives were implemented to raise money. One such made its first appearance in the Lord Mayor's Parade in London, in November of the previous year. This was the Tank Bank. There were two types of tank being used by the Army during the war: the male, with two 6-pounder guns; and the female, armed only with machine guns. Six Mark IV male tanks – *Egbert*, No. 141, *Nelson*, No. 130, *Julian*, No. 113, *Old Bill*, No. 119, *Drake*, No. 137, and *Iron Rations*, No. 142 – toured England, Wales and Scotland in 1918, raising millions of pounds through Tank Bank Weeks.

Tank Week for Sunderland commenced on 22 January, with a special concert and public meeting at the Empire Theatre in the evening. The tank that arrived at Monkwearmouth Station was No. 130, *Nelson*, and it was greeted by the mayor and mayoress. It then proceeded across the Wearmouth Bridge to the town hall, led by the police band, with soldiers on either side. As ever, crowds lined the route to see the marvel, and blind people were allowed to touch these new machines of war. At the town hall the mayor, Brigadier General F.P. English, Colonel Roundell, the Mayor and Mayoress of Durham (Alderman and Mrs Pattison), the town clerk (Mr H. Craven) and others took their stand on top of the tank and addressed the crowd. After a short address the mayor pinned the Military Medal ribbon on 715082 Sergeant P. Docherty of the Royal Field Artillery. Once again, the mayor led the way and invested £50,000 on behalf of the Corporation. Norwich Union Life Assurance followed by investing an additional £10,000. A special area for the Tank Bank was set aside in the Sunniside shrubbery, Post Office Square, where it was open for business. Every twelfth investor, between noon and 1.00 pm, received 15s 6d worth of War Savings Certificates. Temporary offices had been erected for the bank clerks. Bunting was very much in evidence and there was a bandstand for the entertainment of the potential investors.

There was great competition between various towns to raise the most money. Special lighting was set up for the tank and three barometers were erected to show how much Sunderland, Nottingham and Preston had raised. A poll of the money raised was posted up each hour and there were was much cheering when the first million had been reached

AUSTRIAN WORKMEN STRIKE TO ENFORCE THEIR DEMAND FOR EARLY PEACE.

Illustrated Chronicle

ROBERT SINCLAIR

Price One Halfpenny.

No. 2,425 (Registered as a Newspaper)   Tuesday, January 22, 1918.

THE TANK BANK NELSON IN SUNDERLAND: ENTHUSIASTIC WELCOME.

Arrival at the Tank.

Sunderland Orphan Asylum Boys visit the Tank.

(1), The Mayor opens the Tank Bank; (2), A general view of the scene; (3), The Mayor buys a War Bond.

A bit of the crowd.

Nelson's crew.

The arrival of the Tank Nelson at Sunderland aroused great interest. Proceedings were formally opened yesterday morning by the Mayor (Ald. Vint), who addressed the crowd from the tank top, subsequently investing the sum of £50,000 on behalf of the Sunderland Corporation. (I.C. photos.)

How Tank Week was reported locally.

Tank Flag given to investors.

at the end of the third day. On Friday evening, Sunderland led the way, but by the next morning Nottingham had overtaken them. The town did not reach the £2 million mark until noon on Saturday. By the end of the week the town had invested £2,347,851, which equated to £15 10s per head of population. At the end of the event *Nelson* left for South Shields and more fundraising.

People had been campaigning hard to raise funds for Tank week and it was thought that afterwards they would be able to relax. This did not last long, for the mayor was shortly asked to undertake more fundraising with the sale of War Bonds and War Savings Certificates for Cruiser Week. Again, visits to shipyards, engineering works and all kinds of factories were organized. Similar to Tank Week, Cruiser Week was launched with a meeting at the Empire Theatre on a Sunday evening. This government appeal was based on a handicap system, depending on the size of the town or city. Newcastle was asked to raise money for two cruisers and Stockton was asked to fund a destroyer. Although the town had raised such a large sum during Tank Week, it still managed to raise a further £307,089 for Cruiser Week, against a target figure of £400,000.

On 23 March, the SS *Shadwell*, built in 1904 by J.L. Thompson and Sons, Sunderland, was sailing from Naples when she was torpedoed and damaged by the German submarine UB50. Thirteen men lost their lives and the survivors were rescued by the French trawler *Albatross.* An Italian trawler stood guard while the rescue was taking place, and was herself torpedoed. After a French patrol boat destroyed the submarine, the *Shadwell* was eventually towed into Bizerta, Tunisia, where she was repaired. The four engineering officers on the *Shadwell* had been killed in the attack, and all came from Sunderland. They were Rowland Simpson (chief engineer), John Thornton Douthwaite (second engineer), John William Williamson (third engineer) and Thomas Woods Jameson (fourth engineer). All are commemorated on the Tower Hill Memorial. The four deck officers, who were also all from Sunderland, escaped. They included Second Officer Arnold, son of the Sunderland harbourmaster.

Due to the shipping losses caused by German submarines during the previous year, in April the Admiralty attempted to disrupt this menace by blocking the ports of Zeebrugge and Ostende, from where the submarines operated. The plan was to sink blockships in the mouth of the rivers. The

Captain William Miles Morant, 7/Durham Light Infantry, killed in action 11 April 1918. He was a solicitor working for the Director of Public Prosecutions and was the son of the chief constable of the County of Durham.

The grave of Able Seaman W.L. Sutherland, killed in action 23 April 1918 on HMS *Vindictive* at Zeebrugge.

Fallen household members are often commemorated on family memorials as well as on the Commonwealth War Graves Commission headstones.

attack took place on St George's Day, 23 April. The attack at Zeebrugge was successful in the positioning and sinking of the blockship; the attack at Ostende failed and had to be repeated in May.

From this attack a unique occurrence for the town took place. This was the funeral of Able Seaman William Leonard Sutherland, who was buried in Mere Knolls Cemetery. It was reported that Sutherland was killed by the last shell fired at HMS *Vindictive* as he

Captain Frederick Cecil Longden, 15/Durham Light Infantry, killed in action 28 August 1918. He was the first honorary secretary of the Durham County Branch of the Boy Scouts Association.

was stepping on board the ship. Sutherland had previously served at the Battle of Jutland in 1916 aboard HMS *Conqueror*. What makes this unique is that the Admiralty contacted Able Seaman Sutherland's father, who was a sergeant in the Borough Police Force, asking if he wanted the body sending home for burial. Normally the dead were buried at sea or on first landing. The cortège comprised men from an artillery battery, based nearby, a firing party and buglers of the York and Lancaster Regiment, members of the Naval Reserve, the police and some of Sutherland's workmates from Austin's Shipyard, where he had worked in the blacksmith's shop.

One of Sunderland's rugby players, Frederick Cecil Longden, was killed in action on 24 August while serving with 15/Durham Light Infantry. Frederick Longden had originally been gazetted second lieutenant in 4/Durham Light Infantry and served in France with 2/Northumberland Fusiliers, being wounded on the Somme. Following his recovery he returned overseas and was attached to the Durhams, with whom he was killed at Miraumont. His chaplain wrote of him:

Our brigade received orders to attack Miraumont, on the Ancre … Dawn, just beginning to break, showed our men that they were practically surrounded by the enemy, who poured in a galling fire from the front and flanks. Seeing that, Capt Longden led his company forward in the most gallant manner possible, leading his men by a good 40 or 50 yards and inspiring them to advance by his coolness and bravery. His voice could be heard from the other parts of the field, shouting out: 'Come on the Durhams.' He was almost on top of the enemy when he was hit in the head by a machine-gun bullet, which killed him instantaneously … But his gallantry, and that of some other officers, was not in vain.

The war had had an impact on Sunderland RFC, with a number of the first team joining the colours. It was not until 1922 when they were able to sign enough fit men to form a second fifteen team. At least seven of those who had originally joined up died during the conflict.

The second Victoria Cross to be awarded to a member of the forces who came from the Sunderland district was won in October. Sergeant William McNally, who was born in Murton on 16 December 1894, worked at the pits until he joined 8/Yorkshire Regiment (Green Howards) on 3 September 1914. The award of the Cross was published in *The London Gazette* of 14 December 1918. His citation reads:

For most conspicuous bravery and skilful leading during the operations on the 27th October 1918, across the Piave, when his company was most seriously hindered in its advance by heavy machine-gun fire from the vicinity of some buildings on a flank. Utterly regardless of personal safety, he rushed the machine-gun post single-handed, killing the team and capturing the gun. Later at Vassola, on the 29th October, when his company, having crossed the Monticano River, came under heavy rifle fire and machine-gun fire, Sergeant McNally immediately directed the fire of his platoon against the danger point, while he himself crept to the rear of the enemy's position. Realizing that a frontal attack would mean heavy losses, he, unaided, rushed the position, killing or putting to flight the garrison and capturing a machine gun. On the same day, when holding a newly captured ditch, he was strongly counter-attacked from both flanks. By his coolness and skill in controlling the fire of his party he frustrated the attack, inflicting heavy casualties on the enemy. Throughout the whole of the operations his innumerable acts of gallantry set a high example to his men, and his leading was beyond all praise.

This was not the first gallantry medal to be awarded to Sergeant McNally; he had won the Military Medal on 10 July 1916, on the Somme, and a bar to the award on 3 November 1917 for bravery at Passchendaele.

Gun Week was opened by the mayor (Alderman Vint) during the first week of November. To help promote the appeal, guns, which had been touring the country, were brought by road from South Shields, being drawn by four caterpillar tractors on two specially constructed motor lorries. A crowd cheered their arrival. The guns comprised

Opening of Gun Week in Sunniside Shrubbery, November 1918.

a 9.2-inch Howitzer, an 8-inch Howitzer, a 6-inch gun, a 4.2-inch Howitzer, a 60-pounder and an 18-pounder. The procession of the six guns was preceded by the band of the Sherwood Foresters, and then the police, the mayor and councillors and Brigadier General Hibbut of Tyne Garrison. The procession left the town hall in Fawcett Street and proceeded to High Street, and then to Sunniside, to the Shrubbery in Norfolk Street. Here the mayor declared the appeal open and addressed the crowd, saying that the war was nearing its end but still the country needed to quash the formidable German might. A last grand effort was needed, so this was no time to slacken the effort. It was estimated that £8 a head was needed to reach the target. Investments had been pledged, which included £54,000 from the North Eastern Railway Company, £25,000 from the National Provincial Bank, £25,000 from Barclays Bank and £25,000 from the Bank of Liverpool. By 4 o'clock that afternoon, £192,428 had been raised. As an added incentive, the town that raised the most money would be awarded the *Egbert* tank for permanent public display. Sadly, this never happened.

The collection for Gun Week ended on 9 November, closing at 8.00 pm. It was declared a success, although the target hoped for had not been reached. With that in mind the town still managed to raise £943,252 11s 6d, which was not a bad effort considering the war had gone on for four years. Of this figure, £883,573 15s was raised through War Bonds and £59,678 16s 6d by War Savings Certificates. The amount invested through the Post Office was an additional £63,849 3s 6d.

At 5.00 am on 11 November, the Armistice was signed in Field Marshal Foch's

railway carriage in the Forest of Compiègne, but it did not to come into effect until 11.00 am that day, giving all sides enough time to inform their forces. Rumours of the impending cessation of hostilities soon became known throughout the country.

In Sunderland a large crowd gathered outside the *Echo* offices in Bridge Street and West Wear Street. Official indication of the Armistice came at 10.40 am and was greeted by loud cheering from those present. A special edition of the *Echo* was published, which was eagerly awaited. The news boys were mobbed as soon as they left the *Echo* office, some not even getting to end of the street before they had sold out. One boy was forced to his knees, the crush of the crowd being that strong. Another sold his editions at two for a penny, thinking it was a double sheet and not a single.

One man who went into the paper's offices to enquire what was happening burst into tears when told the news. His show of emotion, he explained, was because he had four sons at the

Ferdinand Foch, second from right, seen outside his railway carriage in the Forest of Compiègne.

front. Conversely, a soldier went into the office to place notification in the paper of the death of his brother. When told of the events he replied that it was too late for him.

As the news spread flags appeared throughout the town. Buzzers and whistles at the works and shipyards, and from the ships on the Wear, sounded out the news. Men left their work to celebrate. At about noon the mayor addressed the crowd at the town hall, saying that this was one of those times when he could not find the words to express his feelings and no doubt he would make further addresses in the coming days. At the same time he declared a holiday and asked tradesmen to close shops and schools to close. By early afternoon all the principal streets in the town centre were crowded, most people wearing patriotic colours. There were also parades of children from the East End, one dressed and pretending to be the Kaiser being arrested by two older, bigger boys. In Crowtree Road, pandemonium was caused by boys setting off fireworks. The police band played at the town hall and by 4.00 pm there were so many crowds in the town that they were pushing against each other.

After the elation of the armistice, tragedy came to Sunderland late in the year when the influenza epidemic, which was ravaging Europe, arrived in the town. Within a week there were 8,000 reported cases and shortly the death rate would be at a level of 91.2 per thousand. The people were already weakened by four years of war and strife. Added to this, rationing was now at its height, this combination making the situation worse than it would otherwise have been. One of the biggest problems was the disposal of the dead. It was believed that hundreds were lying in their houses, sometimes in the same room as the living. Meetings took place almost daily between the mayor and local undertakers. As a result temporary mortuaries were opened, some being in schools, which had been closed. Joiners from the shipyards were now employed in building coffins, as was the Army. Aid was given to the invalids by the Guild of Help. Milk was difficult to come by, but there were alternatives such as Oxo and other tinned goods. Volunteers were requested to help the sick due to the exhaustion of the trained nursing staff. Another knock-on effect was the increase in orphans. Help was given by the managers of the Girls' Industrial School; part of the school was given over to an orphan asylum. Another potential difficulty to be taken into consideration was the General Election. In order to control the spread of the disease it was agreed that only those meetings previously advertised would go ahead and no door-to-door canvassing would take place. Luckily the epidemic abated with the same speed with which it had arrived.

One problem that arose during the war was that of stranded soldiers and munitions workers who had been left on the railway station while on leave or visiting local hospitals. Early the previous year, Brigadier English had given the issue serious consideration. Originally the railway company had allowed people to use a waiting room, which kept a fire burning during the night, as some soldiers had been found sleeping in shop doorways. Eventually a room was arranged in the YMCA for soldiers. A member of the clergy, usually Reverend J.T. Brown, the vicar of Monkwearmouth, used to patrol the platform every night at midnight. As for the female munitions workers, they were taken to St Agatha's Mission, in Murton Street.

In December the town was visited by what was known as a Mystery Ship. These innocent looking cargo ships had been used during the war to lure German submarines to the surface and then reveal their true colours as a warship. Officially they were known as Q-ships. People were able to visit the SS *Suffolk Coast*, which was tied up alongside the South Dock. One of the visitors was Mayor Vint, who together with an official party, was treated to a guided tour by Captain Harold Auten. The mayor was taken by surprise at the outward appearance of the ship and the crew. Captain Auten gave the order for the crew to demonstrate what they would do if attacked by a submarine. Some of the crew manned the lifeboats, taking with them personal belongings and even pets. When it was assumed that the submarine, purportedly on the surface, was within range, a 4-inch gun sprang up from the main hold. Those in the official party were suitably impressed.

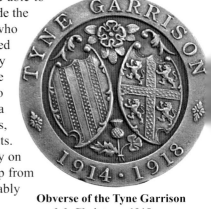

Obverse of the Tyne Garrison medal, Christmas 1918.

The Southwick-built 7,500-ton steamer SS *Sandyford*, launched in 1903, was converted to a Q-ship during the war. She was renamed *Lodorer* and was equipped with five 12-pounders, two 6-pounders and a Maxim gun. Because of a possible leak in security she was renamed again, this time the *Farnborough*, and officially became Q5. On 22 March 1916, she was involved in a fight with the U68 and sank the submarine with gunfire. On 17 February 1917, the U83 also fell prey to her guns.

Reverse of the Tyne Garrison medal, of which Sunderland formed part in 1919.

Chapter Six

1919: Coming to terms and a time to reflect
Peace, parades, memorials and pageants

FIGURES DIFFER AS to the number of men from Sunderland and district who joined the forces during the war. Some say 25,000, other figures suggest 18,000. The true figure is probably somewhere in the middle. Of these numbers it is estimated that about 2,500 men were killed, with many more injured. Personnel were still being classified as 'died in the war' up until the end of 1921.

It was not until late 1920 that the idea of a town war memorial was proposed, although some smaller, more private ones had been erected in churches and places of work. The mayor, Alderman W. Raine, decided to raise the £6,000 needed by means of a Shilling Fund, whereby everyone in the town had the opportunity to make a contribution. Needless to say, the money was soon raised. The design of *Victory*, submitted by Mr Ray, from the School of Art, was chosen and part of Mowbray Park, in Burdon Road was donated by the Parks Department for its erection. A model of the memorial was made for people to see and for blind people to feel. The Sunderland War Memorial was unveiled on 26 December 1922. The local Territorial battalion, 7/Durham Light Infantry, were present, comprising one officer and fifteen men at the base, the band and bugles, and four officers and forty men. The unveiling was by the honorary colonel of the battalion, Ernest Vaux, after the dedication by the Bishop of Durham.

There are a number of other war memorials around Sunderland; some are columns, some slabs, and others have figures on the top, many with names of the fallen. There is even a private one to Gunner James William Rutherford, Trench Mortar Section, Royal

Bishopwearmouth Cemetery Commonwealth War Graves Memorial plot. In addition to this, individual graves are to be found throughout the cemetery.

A private memorial in
Bishopwearmouth
Cemetery to Gunner James
William Rutherford of the
Royal Horse Artillery.

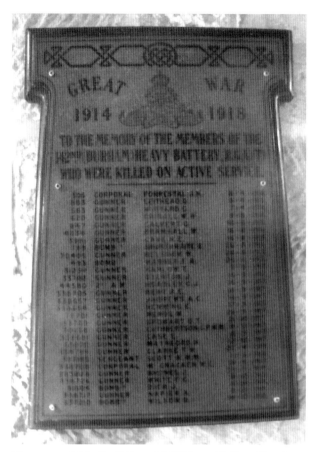

**The memorial to the fallen of 142/Heavy Battery Royal
Garrison Artillery, formerly the 1/Durham Royal
Garrison Artillery Volunteers.**

Field Artillery, who died of wounds received at the
Delville Wood, on the Somme, on 1 August 1916.

Although the war was over, the danger had not yet
gone. On 30 January, a loose mine was washed against
the old pier on Hendon Beach and blew up. This caused
a large breach in the pier, blew out glass from surrounding
properties and loosened roof slates. Luckily, no one was
seriously injured. The mine had, apparently, drifted into a
small cove behind the breakwater, being forced there by
the strong winds and tides. Some men of the River Wear
Commission were working about 60 yards from the mine when it exploded, sending
earth and rocks skywards. They were working in a trench, which protected them from
the blast, but Phillip McCabe was struck on the head by piece of rock. He was not

The new Wearmouth Colliery War Memorial, which was erected in 2008 to replace the original stone memorial that was damaged beyond repair.

seriously injured and was able to walk home later.

The large plate glass window of Messrs Myers Wayman's shop in Suffolk Street was 'smashed to atoms' by the intensity of the vibrations that followed the explosion, but happily no one was injured by the fragments of flying glass.

One of the success stories of the war was the receiving depot, which was under the Red Cross and War Office. The depot was run by volunteers under the leadership of Miss F.O. Huntly, OBE. Originally it started in an empty house with just a sixpence, but by the end of the conflict it had £1,500 annually, raised by donations, flag days and other fundraising events. By the early part of 1917 it had been responsible for the distribution of 118,000 articles of clothing, made by women of the town and sent to men on every fighting front and at sea. Initially it also supplied the needs of Hammerton House VAD Hospital, but gradually was called upon to help with the Belgian refugees, French wounded and refugees, and other

A war workers badge, given to personnel of the Sunderland depot of the War Office and British Red Cross Society.

hospitals within the town. Five hundred special badges were made and issued to workers of the depot.

Many strange things were made and sent to the fighting men, such as paw mittens (made with a slit to withdraw the fingers but leaving the mitten on the thumb and wrist for Lewis gunners). When the war hospital opened, the depot supplied 2,000 articles to it in the first two weeks and 1,000 articles thereafter each fortnight. The depot closed in 1919 and left £100 to enable the work it had begun to continue.

In June a naval detachment, heroes of the Battle of Jutland, steamed into the town, not on a ship but on a train. They had come to promote the Victory Bank in West Sunniside. The sailors were greeted at the station by a guard of honour formed by 3/Devonshire Regiment. Although the weather was slightly inclement, it did not prevent large crowds turning out to see them. The mayor welcomed them and addressed the crowd, stating that although the war was over England still needed its navy, and people were encouraged to buy Victory Bonds. Even after the war had finished the government was still asking towns to raise money for specific causes.

The Wear had a history of shipbuilding, with many years of experience going back to 1346. At the turn of the twentieth century the yards were booming. This lasted until the end of 1907, when work declined, with approximately 8,000 men being laid off. These hard times, before unemployment benefit, lasted only until 1909, when new orders were starting to be placed, and this was the case leading up to the war years.

During 1914, the Wear built a total of seventy-four ships, which made up 319,225 gross tonnage, about a third going to overseas owners.

At the commencement of the war the Ministry of Shipping was established. Existing shipbuilding contracts were only permitted to be completed if the yard in question had the sanction of the Ministry. Another measure was that the resources of the shipbuilding industry were conscripted by the government. Construction of approved types of cargo vessels was allocated to various yards as they became available. This meant that some shipyards on the river built nothing but vessels for the Admiralty, whilst others built a mixture of naval and cargo vessels.

As already established, the shipyards lost men to the armed forces – either Reservists being called up or members of the Territorial Force. The cost of both materials and labour to build the ships rose enormously during the war, as did the cost of living. One result of the manpower shortage was that women started to work in the yards, replacing their menfolk.

Censorship was not fully implemented until 1916. The figures for merchant ships built on the river in 1915 were published in the local press. This was the last time this happened until the war ended. In 1915, thirty-one merchant vessels were built; figures for naval construction were not given. Many of the ships built during the war had the prefix 'War' in their name. It was not until 1917 that standardization of design was introduced into some of the yards. Austin's produced a 'D' type single-deck collier and an 'H' type cargo steamer. Thompsons also produced an 'F' type cargo vessel.

During the war, Doxford's built twenty-one torpedo boat destroyers, whilst other yards dealt with other smaller naval craft such as sloops, patrol vessels and troopships, to name but a few. The following is a list of some of the naval ships built in Sunderland shipyards during the war. Bartram's built patrol boats P23 and P41. R. Thompson built patrol boats P28 and P49. Sunderland shipbuilders built two Insect Class river boats: HMS *Mantis* and HMS *Moth*. Doxford's built HMS *Norseman, Oberon, Octavia, Opal, Ophelia, Opportune, Oracle, Orestes, Orford* and *Orpheus* (all M Class); HMS *Recruit, Redoubt, Ulysses* and *Umpire* (all R class); HMS *Shamrock, Shikari* and *Success* (all S Class); and HMS *Vega, Velox, Walpole* and *Whitley* (all V and W Class ships).

HMS *Redoubt* took part in an action against German shipping in the Heligoland Bight in August 1918, when it towed a barge that carried a Sopwith Camel. The pilot of the aircraft later shot down the Zeppelin L53; both he and his aircraft were recovered from the sea. HMS *Whitley* and HMS *Velox* both saw service against the Bolsheviks in 1919, and also in 1919 HMS *Success* was transferred to the Royal Australian Navy. On 10 September 1918, the German U-boat UB83 was sunk by HMS *Ophelia*.

The fate of Sunderland-built ships

Ship	Launch date	Fate
HMS *Opal*	11 September 1915	Wrecked 21 January 1918
HMS *Opportune*	20 November 1915	Sold for breaking 7 December 1923
HMS *Oracle*	23 December 1915	Sold 30 October 1921
HMS *Orestes*	21 March 1916	Sold 30 January 1921
HMS *Orford*	19 April 1916	Sold for breaking 1 November 1921
HMS *Orpheus*	17 June 1916	Scrapped 1 November 1921
HMS *Octavia*	21 June 1916	Sold for breaking 5 November 1921
HMS *Norseman*	15 August 1916	Sold 9 May 1921
HMS *Oberon*	29 September 1916	Sold for breaking 9 May 1921
HMS *Ophelia*	13 October 1916	Sold for breaking 8 November 1921
HMS *Redoubt*	28 October 1916	Sold for breaking 13 July 1926
HMS *Recruit*	9 December 1916	Sunk 9 August 1917
HMS *Ulysses*	24 March 1917	Sunk in collision 29 October 1919
HMS *Umpire*	9 June 1917	Sold 7 January 1930
HMS *Vega*	1 September 1917	Sold for scrap 4 March 1947
HMS *Velox*	17 November 1917	Sold for scrap 18 February 1947
HMS *Walpole*	12 February 1918	Sold for scrap 8 February 1945
HMS *Whitley*	13 April 1918	Beached 19 May 1940, later sunk by HMS *Keith*
HMS *Success*	29 June 1918	To Australia (*Success*) June 1919
HMS *Shamrock*	26 August 1918	Scrapped 23 November 1936
HMS *Success*	June 1919	From UK (ex-*Success*) June 1919. Sold 4 June 1937
HMS *Shikari*	14 July 1919	Scrapped 4 November 1945

HMS *Whitley*, a W Class destroyer built at Doxfords.

HMS *Walpole*, another W Class destroyer built at Doxfords.

By 1918, the resources of the shipyards were aimed at producing standardized merchant vessels rather than naval ships. During most of the war years there were fourteen shipyards on the river, but in 1918 two new yards were built, the Elgis Shipyard and the Wear Concrete Building Company. The keels of three merchant vessels were laid at the Elgis yard and three for ocean-going tugs at the Concrete yard. These ships were not completed until mid-1919. The Wear Concrete Building Company was situated between Southwick and Castletown. Due to the shortage of steel the Admiralty placed orders for a number of concrete vessels, but as the war ended in 1918, only three were completed (in 1919). These were the *Cretehawser*, *Creterope*, and *Cretecable*. Of the three ships, *Creterope* was dismantled in 1925, *Cretecable* was wrecked off Whitburn in 1920, and *Cretehawser* worked for the Crete Shipping Company Limited from 1922 until 1935, when she was sold for scrap. She was bought by the River Wear Commissioners in 1936 and dismantled to be used as an emergency breakwater. However, in 1942 she was beached at Claxheugh Rock on the river Wear and can still be seen today. She has become a home for seabirds and favoured subject for local camera clubs.

With the end of the war controls were lifted and the yards returned to private contracts for new ships. Once again there was a boom period, with replacements for losses during the war being ordered. As well as this, ship-breaking was also doing well, with many older warships coming to the river for dismantling. One such vessel was the submarine

***Cretehawser*, a concrete barge built in 1918.**

C1, which had originally been destined to take part in the Zeebrugge Raid of April 1918 but, owing to problems, submarine C3 was used in her stead.

The Mercantile Marine had its share of casualties during the war. The following ships were sunk just off the entrance to the mouth of the river Wear:

Name	Date of Sinking	Situation	Cause
Saga	1 August 1915	From Marseilles to Tyne	Torpedoed by U28
Zeeland	1 August 1916	On a voyage from Methyl to Rouen with a cargo of coal	Sunk by UB39
Ravensbourne	31 January 1917	On a voyage from Newcastle to London, two killed	Struck a mine and sank
Presto	6 April 1917	In ballast from London to Newcastle, four killed	Struck a mine and sank
Poltava	19 April 1917	On passage from the Tyne	Struck a mine laid by UC44
Hebble	6 May 1917	Scapa Flow to Sunderland	Struck a mine laid by UC32
Maindy Bridge	8 December 1917	En route from Middlesbrough to Tyne	Torpedoed by UC49
Samso	1 May 1918	En route from Denmark to the Wear	Struck a mine laid by UC49
Sunniva	28 June 1918	On passage from London to Tyne	Torpedoed by UC17
Staithes	21 September 1918	Carrying iron ore, destination unknown	Torpedoed

Sunderland maintained the following six Volunteer Aid Detachment hospitals during the war:

Unit	Location	Present status
3rd Durham VA Hospital	Hammerton House, 4 Gray Road, Sunderland	Private residences (building extensively modified)
4th Durham VA Hospital	Jeffrey Hall, Monk Street, Monkwearmouth	Demolished
11th Durham VA Hospital	Social Centre, Sunderland	Now the Royalty Theatre
20th Durham VA Hospital	St Gabriel's Institute, Kayll Road, Sunderland	Church hall
21st Durham VA Hospital	Herrington Hall, West Herrington, Sunderland	Demolished during the 1960s
25th Durham VA Hospital	Ashburne, Ryhope Road, Sunderland	Incorporated into Sunderland University Department of Arts and Design

The site of the 11/Durham VAD hospital at the Social Centre, now the Royalty Theatre.

Hammerton House, formerly the 3/Durham VAD hospital.

Ashburne House, the site of the 25/Durham VAD hospital, now part of Sunderland University.

St Gabriel's Church Hall, which housed the 20/Durham VAD hospital.

Jeffrey Hall VAD Hospital Medal. This was designated 4/Durham VAD hospital, now demolished.

Commemorative plaque in St Gabriel's church hall.

The hospital at Ashburne House, Ryhope Road, treated 1,493 men during its career, its last admission being on 12 May 1919. Of the women who worked in the hospitals, only some of the kitchen staff, those working in the stables and qualified nurses were paid; the rest were unpaid volunteers. St Gabriel's Hospital received its first wounded on 24 May 1915; the first commandant was Dr G.E. Pearcey, helped by Matron Mrs Cryle, and Mrs Morris as quartermaster. In 1917, additional accommodation had to be erected between the church and church hall, comprising an isolation ward, bathrooms, etc. The hospital closed on 31 December 1918.

The following awards were granted to members of the Volunteer Aid Detachment at the end of the war:

VAD member	Status	Award
Ballingall, Miss Connie	Lady Superintendent and Matron, 4th Durham Auxiliary Hospital, Jeffrey Memorial Hall, Sunderland	Royal Red Cross 2nd Class
Cuthbertson, Miss Margaret Sharpe	Sister, 4th Durham Auxiliary Hospital, Jeffrey Memorial Hall, Sunderland	Royal Red Cross 2nd Class
Dillon, Miss Nora Grace	Commandant, 25th Durham VA Hospital, Ashburne, Sunderland	Royal Red Cross 2nd Class
Rogers, Mrs Elizabeth Louisa	Nursing Member, 11th Durham Auxiliary Hospital, Sunderland	Royal Red Cross 2nd Class
Shield, Mrs Margaret	Matron, 20th Durham VA Hospital, St Gabriel's, Sunderland	Royal Red Cross 2nd Class
Streatfield, Mrs Evelyn Olive	Commandant, Hammerton House Auxiliary Hospital, Sunderland	OBE
Vaux, Mrs Emily Eve Lellam	Late quartermaster, Hammerton House Auxiliary Hospital, Sunderland	MBE
Vaux, Mrs Mary	Matron and Commandant, 21st Durham VA Hospital, Herrington Hall, Sunderland	Royal Red Cross 2nd Class

County of Durham VAD workers medal.

Medal awarded to VAD workers in County Durham.

Reverse of VAD workers medal presented to 439 M. Maule.

Certificate awarded to VAD workers for their services during the war.

Another person from Sunderland to be honoured was William Mills, who was knighted in 1922. William Mills had been born in Southwick in 1856. Mills opened a munitions factory in Birmingham. He was aware that the grenades used by the Army at the commencement of hostilities could do with improving. After research he invented his own grenade, the Mills bomb, which had a central spring-loaded firing pin and spring lever, which was kept in place by a pin. More than 75 million Mills bombs were supplied to the British and Allied armies during the war.

One firm, Speedings, a ships' stores merchant whose business of supplying canvas to the Navy for its ships and to the Army for webbing had increased in the war years, gave their workforce a gratuity at the end of the war. Each male employee received ten shillings and its women, five shillings. Foremen were awarded £2, and forewomen £1.

The year of 1919 was a time for celebration also and on 19 July, a parade took place in Sunderland. Shops shut, trams did not run and work places closed for the day. A holiday atmosphere descended on the town, with crowds gathering early. The parade was a great success for all concerned and it was estimated that it took half an hour to pass any given point and three hours to complete its route. A platform for wounded Tommies had been erected in front of the museum, with members of the Town Council and other leading residents watching it from a stand in front of the town hall. Most of the windows were crowded with people and some even perched on roofs to get a good view.

The parade was very good-natured. When the special constables passed there were

The museum.

often cries of 'Put that light out'. St George led the parade, dressed in golden armour. On a heavy steed came Victory, wearing a laurel wreath, with her four handmaidens, Faith, Freedom, Justice and Wisdom. England came next, accompanied by various characters from history. Scotland followed, carrying her flags in wing fashion, and she was followed by Ireland and Wales, respectively. Each of these characters was paraded on a car. Next to come were members of the Empire, commencing with Canada, Australia, the Union of South Africa, New Zealand and India.

Patriotically, these were followed by Britannia, resting on her sword and accompanied by a sailor from Nelson's time, a Land Girl, a Jack Tar and Florence Nightingale. Following behind these were representations of the Allies, including France, Belgium and Japan, to name but a few. Finally, at the end of the precession came Peace, dressed in pure white and holding an olive branch. To remind people what it was all about, a memorial car to the honoured dead was included, in memory of those who had made the supreme sacrifice. Preceding, between each car and bringing up the rear were civil, naval and military representatives. Mounted police were at the head and brought up the rear of the procession. Units taking part in the procession were: firemen, the Borough Police Band, the police, the mayor and other civic officials, the River Wear Police, discharged and demobilized members of the Royal Navy, the Sunderland troop of the Northumberland and Durham Hussars, the Burns Club pipers, 160 (Wearside) Brigade RFA, Durham RGA, 7/Durham Light Infantry, 20/Durham Light Infantry, 3/Devonshire Regiment (stationed at Castletown), 1/1 Northern Cyclists Battalion and the Sunderland Company (Northumbrian Divisional Train) Royal Army Service Corps. Next came ninety special constables and representatives of local institutions. Of the fifty-man

Memorial car, Peace Procession, July 1919.

A model Zeppelin followed by Britannia in the Peace Procession.

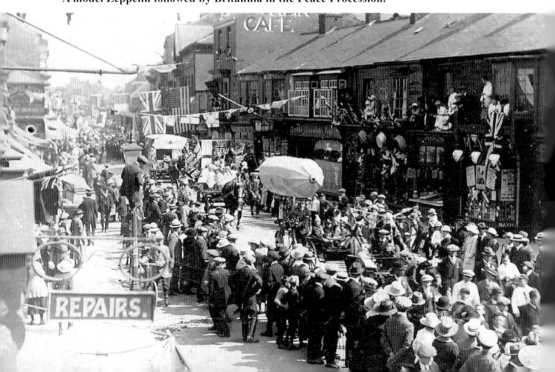

The Peace car, followed by the Girl Guides.

Mercantile Marine contingent it was noted that one man had been torpedoed or mined no less than six times, two, five times, three, four times and the others once or more. A souvenir programme was produced, which also listed schools and individuals who took part.

Various impromptu parades sprang up in the East End, especially involving youngsters. One such scene depicted a Tommy dragging along another lad dressed up as a pitiful, hang-dog-looking kaiser with a halter around his neck. Tea parties took place in the streets, with dancing on the Town Moor and Mowbray Park.

In the afternoon there was a football match at Roker Park, watched by 10,000 spectators. In addition to this there were other sporting activities taking place around the

Discharged and demobilized members of His Majesty's Forces.

The Gallant Durhams.

town, watched by many. Along the seafront, people were being entertained by bands and, in the Garrison Field, a fair drew big crowds. The picture houses and theatres were crowded and there was dancing in the streets.

At 9.30 pm, an illuminated tramcar left the depot in Hylton Road and travelled to Fawcett Street, the docks, Fulwell, Southwick and Chester Road before making its way

The Mercantile Marine detachment represented by a body of seamen and a car carrying models of ships preceding the Boys' Life Brigade and Bugle Band.

The America car with the Sunderland Corporation Tramways Band in attendance and the Japan car in the background.

Boy Scouts in the Peace Procession.

The Peace Procession passing the town hall.

Girl Guides and the Mercantile Marine passing the Londonderry Hotel.

Sunderland constables in the parade.

The Peace Procession passing down a well-decorated Fawcett Street.

back home. The car was greeted warmly wherever it went. It took 860 bulbs to make the design of a small castle. On the sides of the tramcar were stained-glass windows with a shield bearing the inscription Peace with Honour. Ivy leaves were also displayed along the car and small flags flew from the trolley boom.

The mayoress presenting sports prizes to school children as part of the peace celebrations.

A reception for returned soldiers from local units held in the Victoria Hall.

The obverse of the Sunderland Peace Celebration Medal, which hung from a red, white and blue ribbon and was made of a white metal.

The reverse of the Sunderland Peace Celebration Medal, showing a soldier, sailor and aeroplane.

Sunderland Special Constable Patrol badge.

Alderman W.F. Vint, who wrote *A Mayor's Note Book* **recalling his wartime service to the town of Sunderland.**

Of the special constables who had enrolled from 1914, 1,130 men had been sworn in by the end of the war; there were still 670 serving on 21 February 1919. Initially they were to help in emergencies and undertake patrol work, ensuring lights were out if there was the risk of an air raid. However, due to the number of police officers enlisting to fight at the front the specials were needed to do beat work, once or twice a week. It was suggested that specials be given 'a tangible recognition' of their work for the town but it was thought that they already had the reward of keeping Sunderland safe.

The mayor (Alderman Vint) sent the following message, which was published in the local press:

> May I take the earliest opportunity of conveying thanks to all who assisted in making the Celebrations such an unqualified success.
>
> The Symbolic Pageant will cause the end of the Great War to live long in the memories of the younger generation, and the way the entertainments to young and old have been carried out is beyond all praise.
>
> I venture to say that the Town recognized the result of the hard work of the organizers and fully appreciated the way the representatives of the Naval, Military and Civil life took part.
>
> 'Act well your part; there all your honour lies' appeared to be the keynote from the first meeting of the Committee to the beat of the drum.

What of the units raised in Sunderland and district?

The **Sunderland troop, B Squadron 1/1 Northumberland Hussars** went to

Belgium on 5 October 1914, as part of 7 Division, landing at Zeebrugge. They were the first Territorials to go into action, having a skirmish with the Germans outside Ghent on 10 October. From then on they were continually in action until the end of the First Battle of Ypres, in November 1914. After that they were mainly used as infantry until the closing stages of the war, when cavalry actions again took place.

The **160 (Wearside) Brigade, RFA**, raised in early 1915 under the command of Colonel C.W.P. Barker VD, moved from Houghton-le-Spring to Featherstone Park, Haltwhistle, to commence training. Later in August it joined 34 Division and moved to Salisbury Plain, moving into barracks at Tidworth. Lieutenant Colonel W.M. Warburton took over command in December and the brigade crossed to Le Havre on 9 January 1916, just ten months after recruiting had started.

On 14 February, the brigade moved into the gun line, taking over the guns of 23 Division between Bois-Grenier and Armentières. The brigade took part in the Battle of the Somme, supporting 101 Infantry Brigade on 1 July and remaining in action until relieved on 21 August. The brigade later took part in the Battles of Arras and Third Ypres.

During the German offensives of early 1918, at times the brigade had to defend its position with rifle and Lewis guns and some batteries were firing over open sights. Lieutenant W.P. Walker brought his teams into Croisselle during one afternoon and withdrew both his guns, when the enemy was occupying the other side of the village. Major J.A. Young returned after dark to no-man's-land to retrieve all his guns from in front of the enemy.

The brigade was in action almost until the Armistice, and at times it was under French command. On 11 November, the brigade was in reserve in the Vichte area and later became part of the Army of Occupation in Germany. About six officers and 150 men that originally went overseas with the brigade were still serving with it at the end of the war. The battery was awarded one Companion of the Most Distinguished Order of St Michael and St George, four Distinguished Service Orders, three bars to the Military Cross, seventeen Military Crosses, six Distinguished Conduct Medals, seven bars to the Military Medal, eighty Military Medals, and six Meritorious Service Medals, as well as twenty-three foreign decorations and a number of Mentioned in Despatches.

The **First Durham Heavy Battery**, later to become **142 Battery (Durham) Royal Garrison Artillery**, were not at camp when war broke out. After assembling they immediately moved to Cleadon Hills with whatever equipment they had to hand, their job to defend the coast. In November 1915, a Zeppelin paid a visit to the Tyne and it was thought that the barrage put up by the battery kept it from attacking Sunderland.

The battery then moved to Woolwich, where it was equipped with new 60-pounder guns, and on 22 March 1916 it proceeded to France, moving to Kemmel Hill in Belgium. One of the first things it had to do was hand over its new guns and take over those already in position of the unit it was relieving. Its first action was assisting the Northumberland Fusiliers attack at St Eloi. The battery took part in the Battle of the Somme, taking up positions in Sausage Valley, where it helped in attacks on Le Sars and Pozières. The battery then moved to Arras to support the Canadian attack in April, moving forward when the line advanced and the Germans were out of range of the battery. In September at Ypres the battery was at Hell Fire Corner, supporting the attacks on Passchendaele Ridge, where it suffered casualties from shellfire and bombardment.

It then was involved in the German offensives at Ypres and was forced to retire to Zillebeke Road, after which it was withdrawn for a rest, but this did not last long as it was rushed back to the line to support the 51 (Highland) Division at Merville in April.

The Armistice found the battery near Rejet-de-Bailleul. During the war the battery won two Military Crosses, one Distinguished Conduct Medal, ten Military medals, three Meritorious Service Medals and one Croix de Guerre. It suffered twenty-nine fatal casualties.

The local Territorial Force battalion, **7/Durham Light Infantry**, were at camp in Conway, North Wales, when war broke out and were rushed back to Sunderland to guard the coast. In October 1914, the men were asked if they wished to volunteer to serve overseas, and the majority did. Following training throughout the winter of 1914/15, the battalion set sail for France on 19 April. Instead of the normal introduction to the war the battalion was rushed to the front to help stem the German advance during the Second Battle of Ypres, seeing action on 26 April. The battalion took heavy casualties in the action on Whit Monday 1915. Following this they then went to a quiet sector to be instructed in trench warfare.

On 15 November 1915, the battalion became the pioneer battalion for the division and remained so until mid-1918. The battalion saw action in all the major battles, often being one of the last units of the division to leave the fighting zone. Like the rest of 50 Division, the battalion was involved in the three major German offensives of 1918, and by May had virtually ceased to exist. Accordingly, the battalion absorbed the 22/Durham Light Infantry and became the pioneer battalion of 8 Division, where it remained for the rest of the war.

Sherwood Foresters at Sunderland.

Colonel Ernest Vaux commanded the battalion for the majority of the war until April 1918, when he had to return to England for an operation. His place was taken by Lieutenant Colonel A.H. Birchall, who had served with the battalion in 1915 as a corporal. The battalion was awarded the following decorations, some earned with other units: one Companion of the Most Distinguished Order of St Michael and St George, four Orders of the British Empire, one Distinguished Service Order, twenty Military Crosses, one Distinguished Flying Cross, nine Distinguished Conduct Medals, thirty-four Military Medals, ten Meritorious Service Medals, twenty-six Mentioned in Despatches and a number of foreign decorations.

The service battalion raised during the war from Sunderland and district was **20 (Wearside) Battalion Durham Light Infantry**, which began its existence at St John's Wesleyan School, Ashbrooke, in August 1915. The battalion continued its training at Barnard Castle and Aldershot before embarking for France on 4 May 1916 with a strength of thirty-two officers and 1,018 other ranks, as part of 41 Division. Of these original men, 209 lost their lives and a further 561 were wounded.

Initially the battalion took over trenches in the Le Touquet area and during a trench raid, which involved 140 men; no fewer than eighty-three were killed or wounded. The battalion then took part in the battles of the Somme, from 15 September onwards, Messines Ridge in June 1917, and later at Passchendaele. In November 1917, the battalion was sent to Italy, seeing action on the Piave before returning to France in 1918.

By the Armistice the battalion was instructing the 108 Infantry Regiment of the American Army, afterwards forming part of the Army of Occupation. During the war the battalion won six Distinguished Service Orders and bars, eight Distinguished Conduct Medals, twenty-nine Military Crosses, seventy-five Military Medals, twenty-two Mentioned in Despatches, One Médaille Militaire, seven Belgian Croix de Guerre, one Belgian Decoration Militaire, eight Meritorious Service Medals and six French Croix de Guerre.

The Sunderland Detachment of **A** and **B companies 1/1 Northern Cyclists Battalion** was mobilized on 4 August 1914 and was sent to guard the coast, from South Shields to Blackhall Rocks. The two companies occupied various sectors of the Northumberland and Durham coast throughout the war. They never served overseas as a unit, although most of the personnel served abroad, being drafted to infantry units.

Lieutenant Colonel K.J.W. Leather, Commanding Officer 20/Durham Light Infantry.

The **Sunderland Company (Northumbrian Divisional Train) Royal Army Service Corps**, being formed in 1908 under Second Lieutenant R.C. Hudson, was mobilized with the rest of the division. Later the company was renamed **No. 3 Company, Army Service Corps**, 50 Divisional Train and saw service in all the battles of the division.

Sunderland and district's contribution to the Great War was high in manpower and financial terms. From a population of 152,000, between 18,000 and 25,000 joined up, with at least 2,500 giving their lives. This is evidenced by more than 150 war memorials within the Sunderland area. The civilian population was involved too, whether by direct involvement as military targets in the terror of the air raids or by the fact that nearly every family lost someone due to the conflict.

Despite the economic constraints of war Sunderland could be justly proud of its monetary contributions, as the mayor proudly claimed: 'Apart from War Loans a sum of over £114,000 [approximately £21 million today] was subscribed for various objects connected with the war up to the signing of the peace. Contributions in war stock bonds

A certificate presented by the town to all returning members of the armed forces.

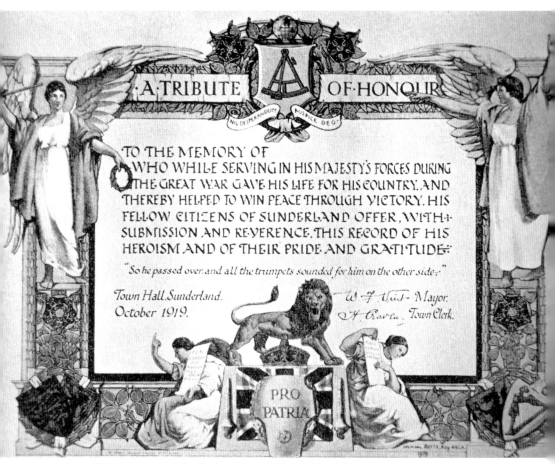

A certificate presented by the town to relatives of the fallen.

and certificates was approximately £15,000,000, or nearly £100 per head of population of 152,000 [today, more than £18,000 per head].'

In the 1918 War Bond race Sunderland was one of eighteen towns that contributed more than £250,000 during the month of October.

Well done Sunderland.

Burdon Road war memorial .

Index